By the same author

UNDERSTANDING DOOMSDAY

CRIME PAYS!

An inside look at burglars,
car thieves, loan sharks,
hit men, fences, and
other professionals in crime

by THOMAS PLATE

Simon and Schuster
New York

Designed by Irving Perkins
Manufactured in the United States of America
By American Book-Stratford Press, Inc.

1 2 3 4 5 6 7 8 9 10

Library of Congress Cataloging in Publication Data

Plate, Thomas Gordon.
Crime pays!
Includes bibliographical references and index.
1. Crime and criminals—United States. 2. Crime
and criminals—Economic aspects—United States. I. Title.
HV6789.P53   338.4'7'364973   75-2052
ISBN 0-671-22058-6

To my close friends,
especially Lesley

Contents

THE CRIMINAL MENTALITY

One day I was having lunch in a typical, dingy New York luncheonette with a contact who makes at least $100,000 a year dealing in illegal drugs. At one point I got up to use the pay phone, which was located about ten feet from the counter. When I got back, I mentioned casually to my contact that not only had I got my dime back but the telephone had returned a quarter as well.

The man bolted up from the soda fountain, ran to the phone booth, and began slamming the side of the phone.

This is the criminal mentality.

CHAPTER ONE

The Ugly Americans

"Some guys go into crime because they are smart."
—A former police intelligence officer

"When you see a guy with a long list of arrests, you know he's probably not a pro. More likely, he's just a jerk."
—A retired East Coast narcotics officer

THEY ARE out there, the quiet ones. Every day we go routinely about our business, and they about theirs. If we are lucky, we never meet.

But, like us, they are caught up in the routine too, rarely making the headlines or the TV newscasts, just doing what they do best, which is making money, picking the right spots, staying away from the law. They are trying to make a success of themselves, in their strange, unorthodox way.

They are our professional criminals.

It used to be believed that all criminals were casualties of society, a sort of class of unfortunates. We believed that the underlying causes were such regrettable factors as a deprived childhood, a weak family structure, a lack of religious conviction, a Y gene, the ghetto experience, an early mistake that snowballed into a lifetime of error—and so on. Indeed, in many circles in the United

States, these remain the accepted explanations for professional crime.

But, as Harvard professor James Q. Wilson, among others, has pointed out, such easy assumptions about crime have little if any basis in solid fact. There is simply no good reason why crime must be understood as the direct outcome of bad housing, unemployment, ghettos, and so forth.

I would go further. It is my hypothesis that professional crime, as we will define it, is divorced from these factors.

Professional crime is the deliberately illegal pursuit of money along well-defined lines. The cause of *professional* crime is not just the criminal's desire for money, but also the surfeit of it in society. It is not the lack of financial and material resource that is behind professional crime in the United States; it is the visible presence of it.

The two go hand in hand. In societies where resources and money are scarce, so is professional crime. But in the United States, the wealthiest country in the world, the profession is powerful, important and deeply entrenched.

Professional crime is primarily a money crime. This is its essential character. For the professional criminal—whether white, black or brown, immigrant or native-born, child of middle-class or of poverty—the motive force is business; *green* is beautiful.

Professional crime is not radical violence, sex crime, or violence for violence's sake. The vicious beating of some old lady for the change in her handbag is not the quintessence of professional crime. Neither is the pointless assassination of random victims by a sniper on top of a university tower. These sorts of crime are the handiwork of amateurs, psychopaths, adventurers—not professionals.

A great deal of crime in America is *disorganized* crime. It arises out of frustration, spur-of-the-moment impulse, recklessness and, above all, thoughtlessness.

By comparison, professional crime is *organized* crime; the acts are those of calculation, tradition and, occasionally, seasoned opportunism.

The professional-criminal tradition in America dates back to Prohibition and extends profitably into the present. Along the road to riches professional criminals acquired a vast arsenal of profit-making techniques. They have improved, expanded and refined these techniques. From their perspective they have constantly sought to advance the state of their art.

Professional criminals are participants in a well-defined world. This is the so-called racket world, and its activities include illegal gambling, bookmaking, loan-sharking, hijacking, robbery, burglary, receipt of stolen property, sale of same, financial frauds of all sorts, narcotics, extortion, and political and police corruption. The techniques of these rackets are generally known to all members of the profession and are regarded as the daily bread of their existence. When a professional criminal gets down to business, he draws on this body of knowledge like a surgeon approaching an operation, or a lawyer preparing for a case.

In the United States there are several hundred thousand professional criminals. No more refined count is possible, for obvious reasons. According to official estimates, crime is a large industry indeed. Loan-sharking, hijacking, and sale of stolen goods are said to be worth $100 billion a year. Drug trafficking is a $75-billion-a-year industry. Illegal gambling brings in at least $50 billion a year.*

The regulation of these industries has spawned the law-enforcement business, and it too is a sizable and costly profession. For

---

* None of these estimates is anything more than an educated guess. This is because the crime business is not well monitored. For one thing, many crimes are not even reported to police; and police statistics, which are the only ones we have, tend to err on the rosy side of the picture. On top of this, many criminals commit acts that are never detected or are not even perceived by the victims as crimes. Some victims are *willing* victims (such as the customer for drugs, women, money at usurious rates of interest, stolen goods); others are simply unaware that they are being taken, until it is too late to do anything about it, at which point the victim, profoundly embarrassed, chooses not to report the crime. For these reasons, the full impact of professional crime on American life is underrated. But whatever the actual numbers, there can be little doubt that the crime business is a major industry in America. It is certainly in the same league as General Motors, a $36-billion-a-year business.

example, the annual budget of the FBI is roughly $435.6 million; that of the U.S. Drug Enforcement Administration $74 million; that of the New York Police Department $1.0 billion. When the budgets of all the various local police, sheriff, public-safety and federal law-enforcement agencies are added together, the total cost of regulating the crime industry must easily approach the size of the Pentagon budget, which hovers annually around $75 billion. In other words, the enemy within is costing us as much as our foreign foes.*

The citizen also pays in other ways. He suffers a burglary, takes out theft insurance, pays higher prices at the meat counter because the meat union is controlled by criminals; he, not the criminal, is footing the bill. As if this weren't enough, the criminal doesn't even pay income taxes on his loot. He leaves the entire burden of government expenditure on the shoulders of the honest man. Perhaps this is the cruelest blow of all.

Seen in this light, perhaps professional crime is not all that bad a business to go into. It may be immoral, illegal, socially mean and rotten—but it may not be an irrational venture by any means.

Nor is professional crime a "problem," in any sense of the word, for the professional criminal. On the contrary, it is the solution to his problem, which is how to make a good living. Professional crime is a problem only for us, the victims and the losers in this war.

We must face up to the fact that many professional criminals go into the crime business because they want to. This shouldn't be too

---

* It is a paradox worth noting, however, that *without* the professional criminal the cost of maintaining these regulatory agencies would be considerably higher. This is because in many areas of the country professional criminals augment the salaries of police, and in some cases possibly attract to the police profession a higher caliber of recruit than would otherwise be possible. Of course, the professional criminal is not paying for better police, he is paying for better police *protection,* in the literal sense of the word. Bribes from professionals also encourage the police to concentrate not on professional crime but on amateur crime—the muggings, rapes, murders, and so forth. In this respect at least, the private interests of the crime profession neatly complement the public's understandable preoccupation with crime in the street.

hard to understand. The pay, after all, can be extraordinary, and the chances of having to go to jail are really not all that great.

This is the great secret of professional crime. If you look at the clearance rate statistics, you see a pattern. The clearance rate is the official police estimate of crimes, by category, which police believe they have solved (whether or not convictions are actually obtained). Year after year, in city after city, the clearance rate shows the same thing. It tells us where the professional criminal is hiding.

At the top of the list is the crime of murder. The clearance rate for this crime, in most places, hovers around 80 percent. This means that four out of five murder cases are solved to the satisfaction of police. This is a high percentage.

At the bottom of the list of crimes cleared are such crimes as burglary, larceny and motor vehicle theft. Here the clearance rate sinks to 20 percent (and often lower). This means that four out of five *reported* crimes are never solved.*

By and large, the professional criminal is huddling near the bottom of the list, in the safe categories of crime. He is purposefully committing crimes in which the chances of getting caught are pretty slim. In this sense, the criminal is not engaging in a high-risk occupation.

There are many professions in the United States that seem to entail much greater risk. Some of them are stuntwork, test-piloting and police work. Even construction work may be more dangerous. According to the Department of Labor, the average construction worker stands at least a one-in-seven chance of sustaining a harmful accident while on the job. Judging from clearance rates—not to

---

* There is another reason why crimes are sometimes not reported. Simply put, the victim may not want the police to know what the criminals took. Doctors, dentists and other professionals whose fees are sometimes paid in cash may hoard a part of their income at home, and fail to report it on their tax returns. When the burglar finds the hidden cache, the last thing the tax evader will do is inform the police, who represent the very government he had been hiding the money from. Another instance of an unreported crime: a burglar stealing from another criminal.

mention the relative ease with which the criminal escapes justice even after a rare arrest—crime may be safer than construction work.

There is, to be sure, some risk in the work, but the risks are regarded as part of the overhead cost of doing business. They certainly are not welcomed and, except for the criminal daredevil, are certainly not enjoyed; they are simply necessary parts of the job.

Many Americans may have trouble accepting this characterization of the criminal. The idea that criminals are irrational deviants is firmly embedded in the mythology of American criminology, history and sociology.

Several years ago, a sociologist came along who devoted considerable research time to the actual lives and attitudes of criminals themselves. He talked to, and even consorted with, known hustlers, criminals and all sorts of so-called deviants. Perhaps not surprisingly, his conclusions differed dramatically from those of investigators whose research was limited to inmates of correctional institutions (as a whole, the profession's obvious losers), or to hypotheses based on previously published works. This sociologist was Ned Polsky, and his conclusion was that professional criminals have perhaps a more accurate sense of what they are about than the myriad commentators who have made a profession out of trying to explain away the phenomenon of professional crime.

Polsky wrote, "When a professional criminal describes himself as being 'like a businessman' or 'just in a different line of business,' the criminologist takes this to be merely a rationalization. It is a rationalization, all right, but it is by no means only that, and often it is not primarily that."

Polsky's point was that the underlying rationale of professional crime, like that of any business, is profit over loss. Everything is geared—to the extent possible—to making money at the least possible cost and risk. If child molesting and rape were profitable rackets, the professional criminal would probably go into them. But they're not, and so he couldn't be less interested.

Perhaps it is unsettling to realize that the crime business is not all that different from any other business in America, whether the grocery racket, the medicine racket, or the educational racket.

By my free use of the word "racket," I am simply trying to make the point that professional criminals are not exceptions to the rule; they are extensions of it. The rule of American life is to make as much money as one can get away with.

The professional criminal may not be a specialist. That is, he may be a burglar one day, a hijacker the next, and a drug dealer the week after that. But, whatever his personal style, the professional . . .

1 . . . revels in anonymity. It is hardly in his interest to make the FBI Most Wanted list, not to mention the Seven O'Clock News. Joey Gallo, who had a seeming passion for publicity and a celebrity status, was the exception that proves the rule. Besides, as one active criminal puts it, where is Joey Gallo today? (The Mafia gangster was, you may recall, assassinated by rival gangsters in a restaurant in Manhattan's Little Italy.)

2 . . . may well be on speaking terms with local police. This is because some local cops front for mobsters, in other instances because cops often rely on active criminals for inside information about underworld activities. Besides this, professional criminals can be *very* understanding about the problems of being a police officer and may try to help out a cop who is sympathetic to the criminal's own problems. Some burglars purposely spread their action around, so as not to confine themselves to any one precinct. This would only embarrass the captain in the eyes of his superiors and perhaps motivate the precinct commander to launch a personal vendetta against the criminal who is the source of that embarrassment.

3 . . . is not necessarily a member of organized crime, although in certain cities and in certain rackets it is a good thing for him if he is. The necessity for a criminal to integrate himself into a formal

crime organization depends largely on the organization's hold on activities in its area.

There is no one all-encompassing criminal organization in the United States. The Mafia comes closest, in that it has traditionally dominated organized crime activities in a number of American cities, especially on the East Coast. But other crime organizations have risen to challenge the traditional predominance of this Italian-American outfit. In the area of international narcotics distribution, for instance, the so-called Cuban and Latin mafias have made tremendous inroads into the racket originally organized by Lucky Luciano, the late Mafia boss of the forties.

In a broader sense, however, most professional criminals *are* functional members of organized crime. This is due to the nature of the business, which often requires a tremendous amount of co-operation among criminals. In narcotics, importers and distributors and dealers have to live together. In stolen goods, the thief and the fence must have an understanding to do business. In gambling, the bookie and the loan shark are intimately allied in the servicing of the customer. In functional ways, then, crime is organized even if it is not Organized Crime.

At the top level of the profession is a loose association of crime bosses known as the national syndicate. As far as anyone has been able to determine, the average professional criminal is on no more intimate terms with the national syndicate than the average government worker in Washington is with the President of the United States. In crime, as in government, there is so much activity that no one central authority can keep on top of everything. "If anybody tells you they know everything that's going on," says one professional criminal in Miami, "you know the guy's a phony. I don't care whether he's a cop, a district attorney, or a Cosa Nostra. This business is too big to keep track of everything. And, actually, who wants to, anyway?"

4 . . . in all likelihood, is not a drug addict. Heroin especially has proven an inappropriate substance for the careful, thoughtful practice of this profession. "You become an addict in this business,"

says one New York narcotics trafficker, "and you're out of business." Heroin users are rarely leading criminals. In one New York Mafia family, one brother, who was not a user, was a top narcotics distributor in the Tramunti crime family. His younger brother, an addict, was assigned menial tasks by the family.

5 . . . tends to take arrests and even prison in stride. The smarter ones actually put some money in a secret savings account for just such an event. However, the better breed of criminal does not get arrested so frequently that he is in and out of prison several times a year.

When prison comes, they look at their unhappy sentence as optimistically as possible. If the criminal is a well-connected member of organized crime, he will often find his friends and associates throwing him a huge going-away party the night before he is to report to the authorities. When the time comes, the criminal tries to rationalize the experience as a kind of paid vacation—room and board, after all, are free. To the extent that the criminal regards himself as a kind of small businessman, he may even be able to understand that, in his line of work, a prison sentence is really just part of the overhead cost of doing business. The theme one hears over and over again in this connection is, "If you can't do the time, don't do the crime."

6 . . . does not leave fingerprints, as every police officer knows. Some wear rubber gloves, some stop at an Army-Navy store on the way to the scene of the crime to purchase a pair of cheap cloth work gloves, which are later dropped off in the nearest storm drain en route home.

When police find prints at the scene of the crime, they are instinctively inclined to conclude that the perpetrator was an amateur (a "Saturday night" thief, in one phraseology).

7 . . . will, whenever possible, run through a crime before actually committing it. In narcotics, a courier might make the scheduled run a day or two ahead of time to see where trouble spots could develop.

8 . . . may be as familiar with the finer points of the law as the

police officer arresting him. Some can recite the Miranda and Escobedo warnings word for word and, in jail, may spend their free
time boning up on the law at the prison library (illustrating one
of the many ways in which prisons serve as sort of graduate schools
of criminology for the professionals). They are also aware of police
clearance rates.

9 . . . may display surprising prudence in the dispersement of income. The best of them avoid conspicuous consumption at all cost,
preferring either to (a) invest their illegally obtained money
through some front, such as a grandmother, or through a shell
corporation; or (b) gamble the score away in a spree in Las Vegas,
Europe or the Caribbean. The point is to make it as difficult as
possible for the Internal Revenue Service to discover that you are
not what you say you are and that you are earning far more money
than you are actually reporting.

Appropriately enough, some professional criminals remain on
welfare rolls even while they are scoring heavily in the rackets. I
recall once sitting in an unmarked police car as an invited guest
on a police surveillance of a known hijacker. The criminal, who
was affiliated with an Italian organized crime family in New York,
lived in a quiet respectable middle-class neighborhood in a two-
story frame house not a great distance from Aqueduct Race Track,
the huge parimutuel thoroughbred gambling institution in New
York City. The hijacker went to the track every chance he had,
usually walking directly to the gate and leaving behind his late-
model Plymouth (and thus not having to pay a parking fee). The
hijacker, a man in his middle forties, had a wife and five kids and,
according to the police, could afford a mistress. He was also a welfare recipient.

10 . . . may be a family man. Although a statistical survey of the
entire criminal population of the United States is not now available
(and never will be), it is my impression that if one could be taken,
it would show that professional criminals as a group have no more
unstable family lives than any other professional group in America.

Of course, it is not uncommon for a criminal with a family to have a mistress (or two) on the side—but this tendency hardly distinguishes him from men in other professions.

Sonny,* who works in Miami and New York, is a professional burglar. He is young (late twenties), hip, and surprisingly well-read. Sonny, with a big red mustache, is also an absolute, unmitigated coward.

This is why Sonny is a burglar. The one thing Sonny hates is people running into people unexpectedly, where one or more of the principals are armed. He says he occasionally has nightmares about it. Despite his nightmares, however, Sonny remains a burglar.

Burglars are the cowards of the underworld. They sneak around hotels, apartment houses and homes in the suburbs like cockroaches in the night, nibbling quietly at private wealth, and scattering into the dark at the slightest disturbance. They are the bugs of the underworld, ever fearful of being snuffed out by the police officer's service pistol or the homeowner's unregistered shotgun.

But this cowardice pays off. It puts the criminal on the very cautious side of the crime business and reduces the possibility of eyewitnesses to the crime. The one drawback is that the burglar must later deal with a fence, since most burglaries yield merchandise rather than currency. But it is a price that burglars are prepared to pay in return for the practice of what they regard as a trade considerably less risky than armed robbery, where the yield is usually cash. Most burglars do *not* carry a dangerous weapon.

The advantages of burglary are best observed in a quick run-through of a typical job. Let us suppose that in this case the target is a luxury apartment house in any major American city.

It is an elevator building, with round-the-clock doorman service and an internal communications system that hooks up each apart-

* "Sonny" is a pseudonym.

ment to a front desk. Despite all this sophisticated paraphernalia, the building is by no means an impregnable fortress to the professional burglar.

The criminal begins the job in his own home, where he carefully chooses his wardrobe. The costume of the criminal is always an important part of his act. In television crime shows, the bad guys are usually attired in vinyl ski parkas and tight black pants with stockings covering their faces. But in the real world, the criminal dresses with only one thing in mind, and that is to look inconspicuous, to look the part not of a criminal but of a legitimate person. Since the target here is a luxury apartment building, it would be a dead giveaway for the criminal to show up in ski parka and slacks.

(Incidentally, there is the widespread belief that criminal taste in dress borders on the carnival. In my experience, the most successful criminals take considerable pride in their appearance, and their taste in clothes approaches that of the average big city homicide detective, which is to say conservatively modish, but not garish. Several fences I know stock certain lines of male dry goods and accessories because of their appeal to their steadiest clientele— detectives and criminals. We should not be surprised that professional criminals tend to dress well. After all, they have the money.)

The criminal is a chameleon. He doesn't want to stand out; he wants to fit in. So, in his own dressing room, he will size up the target neighborhood and choose his wardrobe accordingly. If the target is a nice middle-class neighborhood in the suburbs, or an area of the city filled with luxury apartment buildings, he will dress the part—usually, conservative suit and tie, dark overcoat, hat. He will also carry an attaché case, a kind of status symbol in some neighborhoods, and a reassuring accessory to anyone whose eyes might momentarily wander in his direction.

The attaché case may hold the burglar's tools, but usually, not. This is because the entire arsenal often consists of nothing more than a loid and a set of picks. The loid is the size of a large ruler, and the picks can be conveniently enclosed in a large pipe-tobacco pouch.*

Suitably decked out and equipped, the criminal either drives to within a few blocks of the target area in his own automobile, takes a cab or the subway, or perhaps rents a car for the occasion. One successful burglar who specializes in New York brownstones lives in a ranch house in Westchester County, a suburban area north of New York City, and commutes to work, as it were, on the Penn Central Railroad, often reading on the way to work the *Wall Street Journal*, his favorite newspaper, because of its editorial emphasis on the stock market (in which he is an investor) and on investigative reporting (in which he has an obvious professional interest).

If the target is an apartment building, the first problem is getting past the doorman. I would have thought this would be nearly impossible, but both police officers and burglars with whom I have discussed the fine art of burglary insist that doormen are vulnerable.

One trick is to simply wait the doorman out. When he is preoccupied with a delivery, a resident emerging from a cab by the curb, or an elderly woman with a bundle of packages, the burglar sneaks in.

Another trick is to bluff past the doorman. This procedure employs false credentials, such as an electric company identification card, and some sort of *spiel*. Evidently doormen, who are neither overpaid nor notably skilled labor, are as gullible as the rest of us to the burglar's tricks.

The burglary of a private home in the suburbs is in some ways considerably simpler, because there is no doorman. In this case, the burglar simply makes his entry through the rear door or garage. He will rarely make his entrance through the front door, since this is the opening nearest to the street.

---

* Other possible tools include a lock puller, a bolt cutter, a screwdriver. These standard tools can be purchased at any well-equipped hardware store, though burglars tend not to buy all of them at once at the same hardware store (it might look suspicious). However, most apartment and house entries can be achieved with merely the use of a loid, a set of picks, and a small piece of wood to smash a window, if necessary.

Once inside the house, the burglar will immediately crack open a window. This is a precautionary measure. If during the course of the burglary someone should come through the front door, the burglar has an escape hatch. The moment he hears the jiggling of the keys, the burglar will, literally, fly out the window, even if he's on the second floor.

In the apartment burglary, the criminal will usually dart up the service staircase to the second floor. Then he will take the elevator to the top floor of the building.

A burglar who is not exactly sure what apartment to hit will invariably choose an apartment on the top floor. He reasons that the man who can afford to pay the highest rent in the building is most likely to have valuables contained in his apartment. If the building has a penthouse apartment, for example, the burglar will hit it.

The burglar then picks an apartment with these variables in mind:

1. Is the occupant likely to be out? Quite frequently, the burglar plans his jobs between ten in the morning and two in the afternoon—when the man is likely to be at work, the woman out shopping, the children at school.

2. Is the apartment close to a stairwell or fire escape? If the answer is affirmative, the apartment is ideal. The first thing that the professional has to figure out upon starting a job is how to get out of it very rapidly in an emergency.

3. Is the apartment within view of peepholes? The burglar will choose an apartment least in the line of sight of other apartments. If possible, in fact, he may even tape a few peepholes to avoid being sighted. Curiously enough, cops and robbers I've talked to express amazement that the average resident, looking through his or her peephole and seeing, literally, nothing, will not stop for a second to wonder about what happened to the outside world.

With these variables taken care of, the burglar is now prepared to force his way into the apartment.

First question: Is anyone home? He answers this question in a very direct way. Looking very much like the average door-to-door salesman, he rings your bell. If he hears the slightest movement from behind the door, he heads for the stairwell. If someone answers immediately before he has the opportunity to hide, the burglar will go into an act. He'll explain he's selling magazines, collecting money for a hospital drive, conducting a poll. If the locale is a motel or a hotel, he'll simply stumble as if he had one too many, explain he got off on the wrong floor, and stagger away to the elevator.

But no one is home, no one responds to repeated rings. So now the burglar tries to finesse his way into your apartment. Usually this means breaking down the lock.

Or he may use picks. Picks are small tools that look like dentist's instruments but are considerably less expensive. They are constructed so that at their tips the spring steel, which is hard and well-crafted, hooks back, like a curlicue. The burglar carries various-size picks in a large tobacco pouch, which he hides either in his back pocket or in his attaché case.

Picking a lock is a fine art indeed. I have tried it several times, under the supervision of both police and criminal experts, and I cannot do it. It is more subtle than needlework and requires the patience of Job, but I quickly get annoyed and fumble around pointlessly until my arms and fingers tire from the effort.

The best pick men, one is told again and again, work at it almost daily to maintain their competence. Most are known to keep abreast of the latest developments in the locksmith industry. When a new burglarproof lock is advertised in the newspapers, the criminal goes to the store to buy one to practice on. He will work on it over and over again, until he can pick the lock in a matter of minutes. If he never masters the lock, he'll never try a door that has that lock. (Several firms make door locks that are tough to crack.)

There is even a correspondence course given by a New Jersey company that will teach you the rudiments of locksmith work. Some criminals have taken this course. Others work as assistant to a licensed locksmith to learn the trade. A few pick men are even licensed locksmiths, plying their trade on a contract arrangement for professional burglars. As detective John Kid, an expert pick man for the New York Police Department, once put it, "You have to work on it regularly or you lose your touch. You really have to work very hard at it."

By hook or by crook the burglar is inside your home. "The odds are that the professional will successfully break and enter on more than 90 percent of his attempts," claims one New York private detective.

Maybe there is a light on inside the apartment. Perhaps the tenant believed that leaving a light on would scare away a burglar. Perhaps the tenant is actually home, asleep. Either way, the professional's procedure is identical. In a booming voice, he will shout, "Anyone home?"

If there is, he'll duck out of the apartment and bound down the steps in no time at all. It should be pointed out that the existence of a light burning is absolutely no deterrent at all, despite the advertised advice of many utility companies. For one thing, burglars know that many people fail to turn off the lights when they leave, either in the mistaken belief that the light has a deterrent value, or simply out of forgetfulness. (If you want to scare a burglar, you'd actually be considerably better advised to leave the radio on! The burglar will hear the radio through the front door and in all probability not even bother entering. If you live in the suburbs, you may have been advised that keeping the lawn trimmed while on vacation and stopping the newspaper delivery are deterrents to crime. Actually, no burglar has ever been stopped by a well-trimmed lawn, nor will he even bother checking the front step for newspapers. Remember: he enters through the back way.)

But there is no one home, and so the burglar moves inside. Before proceeding further, however, he may take an additional precaution. He will stick a match or a small sliver of metal into the keyhole before closing the door. With this little device, the burglar jams the keyhole so that should the tenant return while the burglar is inside rummaging around, entry will be impossible; the key won't fit. The burglar will hear the jiggling, which will last until the tenant, confused, gives up and looks for either the doorman or the superintendent for assistance. In that period of time, the burglar, not wishing to take any more chances, will make his escape from the building.

With his rear defenses secure, the burglar then completes the easiest part of all, which is ransacking the home or apartment. His first target is the top drawers of all the bureaus and desks, or a jewelry box, where valuables are so commonly hidden. If there is a hamper in the bathroom, the burglar will poke around in the bottom among the dirty clothes, such an unseemly place being, according to burglars, a very common hiding place; then all the other drawers in the apartment or home; and then, finally, if there is a wall safe, and if the burglar feels he still has time, he will try to crack that.

He will do all he can within the shortest possible time, not wanting to remain inside for more than five or ten minutes. He will not press his luck, because the event he fears above all is the return of the tenant and the possibly ugly confrontation which that might entail.

The professional burglar will probably forgo the big, bulky items, like the color television and the stereo. His priorities will include cash, traveler's checks and jewelry. (Occasionally he will concede the small score for the sake of the big hit. Suppose in the bureau drawer is a few hundred in cash and a book of blank personal bank checks. If the burglar has time, he will try to find a copy of the signature of the tenant in an attempt to cash a few of the checks later that day at the bank. In such an event, he will leave the cash there and try to effect a departure that leaves no indication that the place has been entered. If the name on the check is female, he will have a girl friend or female accomplice attempt to cash a few checks at various branches of the bank—not at the home branch, probably, since the owner of the account may be known to the bank personnel and the impersonation might be exposed. The professional will never withdraw the entire amount, of course, since bank procedures differ in such a case; but more than enough to compensate him for having passed up the quick small score of cash.

The exit routine is rather standard.

The burglar first peers out the peephole to see that the hall is clear.

Then he opens the door and exits back first.

As he is leaving, he will glance down the hall to see if others are watching his exit. If someone is, he will slide smoothly into a verbal con that will go something like this: "Well, it was really good to see you again after all these years. You know, I'll be back in town next week on business. Perhaps we can have lunch. Yes? Fine. I'll call you when I get back to town and we'll work something out."

To anyone looking on, the criminal is a friend of the victim.

And, if the sliver left behind in the lock was metallic, the burglar will effect the withdrawal with a small pocket magnet. Otherwise, he'll simply leave the shoved-in match or toothpick behind.

The burglar leaves the apartment as any other visitor would. He walks out the front door. The doorman doesn't know any better; he didn't see the burglar enter, so he assumes his entrance occurred during the previous shift.

The professional gets into his car, starts it up, and drives away. Usually his first stop is a bar near his own apartment for a good stiff drink. (Some burglars have been known to defecate on the premises of the burglary, thus leaving behind additional unpleasantry. Some experts attribute this behavior to the criminal's disrespect for the victim. In my view, a better explanation is plain, cold fear. Burglars, as I say, are not heroes, and they get very nervous while on a job.)

As you perhaps have concluded, it is generally easier to burglarize a home in the suburbs than a luxury apartment with doorman. The only edge that the suburban homeowner has is his neighbors, who are more likely to look out for the people next door than their counterparts in the city.

What can you do to protect yourself from the professional burglar? The answer is, from the *professional* burglar, not much. My only advice is to make it as difficult as possible for him to enter your home. This means a good lock, a burglar alarm (which is flagrantly advertised as such on the exterior of your home or apartment), and a nice dog who turns into Mr. Hyde in the company of intruders.

The general line here is that the only way to keep the professional from taking you is to increase the cost of his doing business on your premises. This means making him invest more time at your place than he wants. If it will take him ten minutes to get through your door and the burglar is prepared to invest only five, then you are making it all but certain that he will choose another place to enter.

The importance of the time factor in the burglar's thinking should not be underrated. In one celebrated case in Chicago, burglars who got away with nearly four million dollars in cash from an armored-car company left behind more than twenty-one million, even though they knew it was there. The reason was that they didn't have the time to pack off that many cumbersome bundles of cash. As professionals, they took as much as they could under the circumstances, knowing that it would be better to leave safely with the four million than to risk the delay necessary to package the entire bankroll.

Professional burglaries constitute a small portion—certainly less than half—of the total number of burglaries committed in the United States, which were estimated to number 2,540,900, for example, in 1973. However, they do account for a large number of successful burglaries, and most certainly a very high percentage of the big ones.*

When the Paramount Jewelry Exchange in the heart of Manhattan's jewelry market was hit in 1974 by burglars for $1,500,000 in gems, precious metals and cash, the operation had the unmistakable smack of professionalism about it. The burglars broke through the two thick concrete walls, circumvented an intricate alarm system and opened two huge safes without leaving even a smudged fingerprint. They used power drills and sledgehammers to knock through the walls (the burglary occurred on the weekend, when the jewelry district is virtually abandoned), and somehow bypassed the electronic alarm system that covered the basement, all doors and the safes. Opening the safes was evidently no problem. "Whoever did it didn't have to blast, burn or bang the safes open," said one investigating detective. "He played them like twin pianos, tickling the dials until the locks opened."

Investigators believed that this was the same burglary team that the week before had robbed a jewelry firm a few blocks from Paramount of $75,000 in gems. In that operation, the thieves disconnected the burglar alarm, sprayed black paint over the windows, and opened a walk-in safe with an acetylene torch. Police officers also assumed that this was the same gang that hit still another jewelry firm the year before, after knocking out thousands of burglar alarms in downtown Manhattan by cutting cables serving the Holmes Protection alarm system.

The burglary of the Paramount Exchange was the type of job that had to be cleared, or approved, by the powers that be in the

---

* It is, of course, ridiculous to attempt to estimate how many *professional* burglaries are committed each year. Police statistics do not distinguish between amateur and professional jobs, even though police officers in private do make such a distinction in individual cases. Besides, a national figure on professional burglaries would require (1) the establishment of uniform national criteria as to what constitutes professionalism by police agencies at every level, and (2) detailed analysis from the perspective of these criteria on each and every burglary. These requirements are, at this time, simply beyond the scope and capability of most police crime-analysis units.

New York underworld. It occurred in an area whose rackets were under the control of a local Mafia family, and the take was so large that it is inconceivable that the local Mafia would not have demanded a cut of the take in return for certain services.

One of the services provided was a fence, a figure who is the subject of Chapter Four. "A heist this size, and pulled off with such thoroughness and attention to details," said one police detective, "had to be the work of professionals, and they had to have the approval of Gambino."

Carlo Gambino is the boss of one of New York's crime families and, at this writing, the reputed titular head of the Mafia in the United States.

"After all," the detective continued, "where are they going to fence all that stuff? Any fence big enough to handle a million dollars in gems and metals has gotta be known to the family, and a fence who is won't handle a score that size unless he hears from Carlo that it's okay to do so. The fence wants to stay on good terms with the boss, and the burglars want to stay in business. So the burglary had to be approved from the top."

Not all burglaries have to be approved by higher-ups, however. Burglary remains one field where there is plenty of room for semi-independents to maneuver.* This is one of the attractions of the trade.

In 1974 a male-female burglary team credited with burglarizing more than one hundred hotel rooms—some in the better hotels on Manhattan's fashionable East Side—were finally apprehended by police. A tip from an informant led police to a small apartment above a massage parlor.

When detectives approached the door of the apartment, a male

---

* I use the term "semi-independent" because no burglar is completely free of the interlocking mechanisms of professional crime. Even after a score done all by himself, the burglar is often left with the problem of converting merchandise to cash, and for this he frequently turns to the fence, who is functionally connected to the larger web of the crime world through numerous contacts among loan sharks, thieves and crime lieutenants (see Chapter Four).

voice shouted out that he would "blow away" anyone who tried to enter. The detectives called for reinforcements, and later six police officers armed with shotguns burst through the door.

The suspect surrendered without a struggle. He was not, of course, armed. He was a professional burglar.

CHAPTER TWO

The Perfectly Small Small-Business

CAR THEFT is a rather attractive trade for the young criminal, and the organization of a car-theft ring especially attractive to the crime boss. It is, at all levels, an enormously uncomplicated crime. All it takes is a few tools and a lot of parked cars.

It is also a very important one in the United States. If you were persuaded that the film *The Godfather* contained all the basic truths about American crime, then you are likely to be surprised by this chapter.

Car theft accounts for one of the most significant and least-discussed crimes in America. While narcotics and hit men and gang shoot-outs monopolize the headlines of the nation's press, the car thief is quietly stealing your beautiful new car. Then he sells that car to a higher-up in the crime world, who in turn puts it into a professionally organized car face-lifter. When it comes out, it is a car of a different color, perhaps with different accessories, and almost certainly with altered serial numbers.

Actually, the business of stealing cars has just about everything going for it but drama. The thief does not have to pack a gun, the life of the owner is hardly ever endangered (in fact, he's usually behind locked doors fast asleep as the thief slips away with his

valuable property), the police rarely are lucky enough to catch
the thief in the act, and the car-owning public is, after all, insured.
Most car owners carry theft as well as accident and liability
insurance.

But whether the American public is protected from the ultimate
cost of the car-theft business is another matter entirely. For it is
an enormous business indeed. Although hard data to prove my
point beyond debate obviously does not and cannot exist, it is my
belief that the trade ranks in the top five money-makers in the
profession of crime.

Some inferences are necessary. According to the best estimates
of the FBI, in its annual Uniform Crime Reports, approximately
one million automobiles are stolen every year. (This is the *reported*
figure.) Using this rough figure, it can be estimated that the stealing
and fencing of automobiles is a $2-billion-a-year business (gross)
that realizes profits approaching one billion a year.

The inferences are based on the supposition that the average
retail value of a stolen car is $2,500. This is because the car thief's
priority is the late-model luxury car. On this supposition, then, the
figure of $2,500 is a conservative one indeed.

Profit margins are extraordinary precisely because of the low
overhead of the business. As you shall see, it costs the organizer
of a car-theft ring about one hundred to two hundred dollars per
car. This means that if his streetwalkers, as it were, steal a car
retailing on the legitimate market for $2,500, and he sells it to one
of his customers for $1,500, he still clears a profit of more than
$1,000. Once again, my suppositions are very conservatively
hedged.

Let us compare this business with American Motors. American
Motors of Detroit in calendar year 1974 manufactured 351,378
automobiles. Although manufacturer's profit on each car is not
public information, it may be observed that healthy American
corporations are delighted to be able to report a profit of more
than 5 percent or so (10 percent and they are doing marvelously).
But the car-theft ringleader, who invests one to two hundred

dollars per unit and realizes a profit of 1,000 to 2,000 percent, is, at that profit level, doing considerably better than American Motors. Ford isn't the only one with a better idea.

In view of the omnipresence of the auto in American life, it is hardly surprising that the professional criminal is involved. American society is as addicted to the automobile as the American subculture is to drugs, and as Meyer Lansky was once quoted as saying, "it is the business of crime to profit from and exploit human weakness."

The car thieves I know live and work in the New York area. According to the New York Police Department's auto-crime unit, roughly 100,000 cars are reported stolen in the New York area each year. This is 10 percent of the national total. New York, of course, is not Chicago or any other American city. Certain characteristics of this metropolis make the craft of the car thief somewhat different from that of car thieves elsewhere, but the differences are not very important. It would take the professional car thief perhaps all of ten minutes to get the hang of the peculiarities of another locale.

The economics of the business are exceedingly attractive. There is always a market for a stolen car, and the investment capital required to get started is minimal. The tools of the trade are cheap and readily available. Under these circumstances, I wasn't surprised when a New York City detective once said to me:

"You want to go into crime? Okay, I got an idea for you. Don't become a hit man. Too risky. Besides, you might miss the guy and he may be fast on the draw. Holdup man, or hijacker? Dangerous, very dangerous. A lot of average Joes are walking around with pistols in their pockets, just waiting to become heroes. Narcotics? Well, I admit there's a lot of money in it, but the judges are getting tougher all the time. You can spend a lot of time in prison trying to figure out how to spend the hundred grand you've got in a Florida bank account. Hey, I got an idea for you, how

about stealing cars? Nice work, you know, and easy—cars all over
the place. What are your chances of getting caught? Not very
great. Think you'll have much trouble unloading a six-thousand-
dollar Buick Riviera for twenty-five hundred? Not in this country.
Going to have to meet the victim face to face and maybe blow
his head off if he doesn't blow yours off first? No way. Steal the
fuckin' car when he's asleep, or maybe when he's inside E.J.
Korvette's buying discount Venetian blinds. And don't worry about
having to do time if you get caught, which you won't. In this city
[New York] the judge lets you go with a suspended sentence first
few times you get burned. After all, he figures, you didn't shoot
anybody, did you? Just stole a dumb car. You have to be pretty
stupid or unlucky to do time for GLA [grand larceny auto]."

Although a great many car thefts occur in America's cities, this
perfectly small small-business is by no means exclusively an urban
phenomenon. Increasingly, car-theft rings are being put together by
professionals in the nation's suburbs as well.

In Nassau County, Long Island, for example, an alleged seven-
man ring roamed the streets of this prosperous suburb and, in 1972
alone, stole twenty cars (including fourteen Corvettes) at a total
value of $125,000. The head of the ring provided a garage in
Queens, where the stolen vehicles were stripped down and rebuilt
with different parts before they were marketed with forged registration documents. (In 1974, the seven-man ring was indicted; one
of the men was a landscape architect for the Nassau County Department of Public Works.)

Try to put yourself in the position of the professional criminal.
Your job is to make money however you can, without regard for
the law, at the lowest possible personal risk, and with all the profit
you can muster.

You walk down the street of a major city in the United States, and facing you is a fortune in valuable property. The property owners are locked inside their apartments and townhouses, myriad locks and bars protecting their furniture, television sets and personal effects. But outside, on the street, sits one of the most valuable items they own, their automobile. Several thousand dollars of easily disposed-of merchandise lies out there in waiting by the curb, while far less valuable merchandise is given the benefit of the Medico lock, the doorman, the burglar-alarm system, and all the other modern security devices.

The professional criminal finds this precisely to his liking. The professional burglar doesn't even have to commit burglary, the breaking and entering of a premise; the offense is simple larceny, which is an important qualification for a criminal anxious to avoid the possibility of (1) his victim interfering in the act, and (2) a judge coming down hard on the perpetrator. As I say, in the city of New York and in many other jurisdictions around the country, the chances are eight out of ten that on first *conviction* the auto thief will receive a suspended sentence, and perhaps a fine, but will not have to do time; and this is for a crime involving perhaps your most valuable possession.

There are several sorts of car thief. The most common is the up-and-coming criminal novice for whom car thievery provides an easy entry into the underworld. Under most circumstances, the thief will work on orders—specific orders—from some larger ring. He will literally receive a shopping list for what the organization wants. Often the orders will come over the phone. If fuel is tight, the small car may be in demand—especially a late-model sports car, like a Porsche. If fuel isn't tight, the big, splashy luxury cars, like the Cadillac Eldorado, are the preferred items.

Having received his orders, the young car thief heads for the automobile showroom. In New York, Chicago, Los Angeles and other large cities, the thief works the largest outdoor car showrooms in the world, which is to say the streets of the city. In this showroom are parked cars of every conceivable make, model and year. All the car thief has to do is find what he's after.

Having located the car, the thief then has to decide the method of theft.

If the thief is a heroin addict—the lowest form of criminal in the underworld pecking order—he may simply employ the criminal's primary tool of the trade: his fist. He may just smash through the side window, let himself in, try to jump-start the car, and drive away. However, in the process he may alert the entire neighborhood to his presence, the car owner included, so that the professional car thief does not much prefer the fist-through-window method of forcible entry. And professional car-theft ringleaders prefer not to employ addicts unless absolutely necessary; addicts tend to be incompetent and unreliable. Instead, the ringleaders prefer to engage the services of the ever-reliable, hard-working, quiet-as-a-church-mouse, *professional* car thief.

Sometimes the professional car thief is a two-person team. Without one another, the individuals are nothing. The first member of the team is a spotter. Armed with his shopping list of desirable models and makes, he stalks the streets lining up the merchandise. Then he phones in the information, including precise make, model and street location, to either a central dispatcher, who may be conveniently located at an auto-body shop or nearby junkyard, or directly to the man who is going to make the actual removal. The spotter is the advance man who sets things up.

The thief himself will have his own specialized tools. The tools will be contained in an attaché case, or simply within the confines of the professional's clothing. For this purpose, a large, bulky raincoat is especially useful, for on its interior lining can be strapped a variety of tools, and when it is flopping loosely about can hide the machinations of the thief, about which detail will be offered later. One thief I know wraps *The New York Times* around one of his tools. It is entirely possible that the thief has not missed a single edition of this great newspaper in the last two years and yet could not tell you what the inside pages of the paper looked like.

The tools of the trade are similar to standard burglar tools with two exceptions. The first is a set of master keys. These are *not* ordinarily available from your local showroom or auto plant—except for a price. A set of Porsche master keys, for example, might go for several thousand dollars. In fact, in New York a few years ago one professional thief slipped a showroom employee a cool four thousand dollars for three master keys that would open a certain line of late-model car.

Where specialization is not the case, a more forceful way of breaking and entering the car is practiced. The vehicle for this larceny is called the slam hammer. This incredible tool can be purchased at any large tool-and-die outlet and need only be slightly modified for the criminal's purposes. A slam hammer's legitimate purpose is to pull dents out of cars. For this, a movable lead ring weight is employed for the mechanical advantage. At the fat end of the tool is a large screw which is literally screwed into the depressed area of the car's body. Then a mechanism on the hammer is forced outward, much like a corkscrew's two levers sliding down to extricate a cork, and the dent is forced back to its normal position to await sanding and repainting.

The slam hammer that the professional thief uses, however, is designed not to smooth dents on battered cars but to pull cars out of parking lots and side streets. An expert showed me how it was done.

The two of us piled into his late-model Chevy, he with his slam hammer (or "bam-bam," as it is sometimes termed on the street), and I with a vague apprehension that I was about to fail miserably as a car thief. My friend told me that anybody who can open a Castro convertible can slam-hammer his way into a car.

We drove not to the parking lot of a shopping center, where he often worked, but to a junkyard in the city. He was quite friendly with the owner of this establishment, for reasons which will become abundantly clear a bit later, and explained to him that he wanted to show me a few tricks on an old model car.

The owner laughed as he looked at my innocent face but said, sure, why not, go ahead.

My friend set up the operation exactly as he would perform it in a real work situation. We drove up to within a hundred feet of the car to be stolen.

I got out of his car. At his instructions, I was wearing a large flappy raincoat that successfully hid the slam hammer from view.

I went over to the junked car as though I had known this car all my life. Nothing in my actions, my expert friend pointed out, ought to suggest that I was anything but the owner of the car. From a distance, it looked as though what I had done was to go over to the passenger door, look in the window to make sure the door was locked, and then leave a few seconds later.

Actually, what I did was to go over to the lock on the forward passenger-side door, insert the screw end of the slam hammer, and in a matter of seconds extract from the door the entire door lock. The reason for choosing the passenger-door lock, my friend explained, was that even if the owner of the car returned, he would most likely enter the car on the left side and drive away without noticing the missing lock on the right side. On the other hand, were the driver's door lock to be popped, he would certainly notice and almost certainly let out a howl, perhaps attracting the attention of police.

Next, with the lock still dangling from the end of the slam hammer, with the bam-bam cloaked by my flowing raincoat, and with my self-confidence tremendously boosted by the successful extrication of the lock, I casually but quickly sauntered back to my "partner." Inside the car, I removed the car lock from the end of the slam hammer. My partner in simulated crime then took out of his attaché case a Curtis Auto Key Code Book and his portable Curtis Key Cutter.*

On the car lock now in my possession is etched a code number. Every lock, so far as I am aware, has a code number on it. It indicates to the locksmith how to make a key that will fit the lock.

_____

* I should mention that only licensed locksmiths are supposed to possess these key cutters, but somehow they frequently find their way into the wrong hands.

This is tremendously useful information to a locksmith if you are locked out of your car or apartment. It is also tremendously useful to a car thief if he is locked out of your car.

I read the numbers off to my friend, who started to cut the key himself but then thought better of it. He wanted me to go through the full experience to see how easy his job was.

I inserted a blank key into the Curtis Key Cutter, which is about as large as an average pair of gardening shears but somewhat lighter in weight. On the cutter are various markings for the different depths to which you would want to cut the blank key in order for it to match the shape of the original. These markings have numbers on them (1,2,3,4, et cetera) and color codes (green, yellow green, red, and so forth). The appropriate marking is entered in the Curtis Auto Key Code Book. The markings correspond to what kind of blank key is used and how the key is to be cut.

In about two minutes (maybe three or four) I had a key to fit the door and ignition of the car. I knew this, because once I had the key cut, I tried it on the lock in front of me. It moved the tumblers. Any key that moves the tumblers of the door lock is going to work on the ignition.

Then I got out of the car and went to the junked car. I walked as though I had walked to this car all my life. After all, I had the key, I must be its owner.

Putting the newly cut key into the lock, I opened the car door, got behind the wheel, and put the key in the ignition. If the car had not been in this junkyard in New York minus its motor, I would have started the ignition and driven it out of the parking lot, probably even waving to the attendant at the exit.

Then, according to my crime professor, I was to drive this car to a drop-off spot a few miles away, leave the keys in the ignition, and walk away from that car forever.

For less than an hour's work, I would have earned a hundred dollars, as minimum payment. This is the going rate for the professional car thief in most places. Sometimes it is more. Special orders bring special rates. It is never less (unless the thief is a junkie and works for fixes instead of cash). A hundred dollars for an hour's work is really good pay. Some lawyers make considerably more for an hour's work, of course, but it is only the lawyer who must endure an average of seven years' higher education, not to mention the daily commuting to the office. Many criminals claim to be absolutely allergic to working in an office.

The stolen car now sits in a parking lot. Parking lots in shopping centers are favorite drop-off points for car thieves. Indeed, shopping centers are preferred drops not only for car thieves but for a wide variety of criminals engaged in the transfer of contraband.

The stolen car may sit there for several hours. But it won't be left there overnight. Police patrol cars routinely check parking lots at night for abandoned cars, back seats filled with loving couples, and drunk drivers sleeping off their excesses. Leaving a stolen car in a lot overnight is not considered smart business.

In due course the organization will dispatch a runner to pick up the car. The runner will work for the ring as a kind of odd-job man. He may even be the "gopher," the guy who goes out for coffee and Danish when he's not running after stolen cars. The point of using the runner is to insulate the higher-ups in the ring from the street-level thief who actually stole the vehicle.

The street thief, who several times a week may be receiving envelopes filled with cash at a local bar, will probably not even know the identity of the ringleaders. He will never have met them. If the street thief is picked up by police in the act, he will actually have very little to tell them about the organization. All he does is steal the car, drop it off, and collect a few days later. Payment may be in the form of hard currency (usually one hundred, or perhaps two hundred, if a special order), or narcotics, if the thief is a user (one of the more important reasons for organized crime's involvement in narcotics traffic is to provide chemical currency with which to pay off crime workers).

If and when the thief is picked up by police for questioning (chances are he never will face this problem), his response is textbook ignorance: "This guy Louie, he calls me and says he wants this or that. So I go do it. Then I drop the car off, wait in a bar, and another guy I never seen before comes in and gives me the bread."

And, since this is the way most car-theft rings are organized, the criminal's statement to the police officers will be entirely truthful.

The stolen car is now in the hands of the ring. It is still a hot car. Perhaps by this time the police even know that it is hot. The owner may have detected his vehicle's absence and, if he himself hadn't purchased the car from a dubious entrepreneur, have reported the loss to police. For its part, law enforcement will enter the vehicle's plate and vehicle identification number (VIN) on their so-called hot list. This is a lengthy compilation of cars reported stolen. In some states, because of the daily volume of thefts, the list is compiled by computer and updated on a round-the-clock schedule. In New York City, some patrol cars are being equipped, at this writing, with computer consoles so that the process of checking out possibly stolen cars will be instantaneous. This new system will present problems, but the professionals will get around it by removing the hot car from the streets immediately and not putting it back in circulation until the relevant identification marks have been erased.

However, some rings have been known to slap a new set of license plates on the car and let it go at that. Where do they get the plates, besides off another car?

In the United States, as of this writing, you could write to the Alabama Department of Motor Vehicles for plates. The requirements are that you provide this state agency with a description of the car, the vehicle identification number, and a registration fee. The state of Alabama does not send a representative out of state to check on the veracity of the application, and apparently is willing to provide plates as long as you provide the relevant information and, as I say, some money. Alabama Motor Vehicles maintains an inadequate watch over the integrity of the applications it receives and processes for out-of-state money. No effort is made to thwart criminal exploitation. After all, you could send the state of Alabama a description of the car that hasn't even been stolen yet. Then, when the plates arrive, your men can go to work.

In the city of New York, however, any automobile bearing Alabama plates is immediately suspect by police—I should say, by those few police sufficiently informed about the tricks of the trade. So some criminals add one more step to the process, which really involved the "laundering" of motor vehicles. ("Laundering" is an underworld term describing a process designed to hide the origin of a piece of merchandise. Usually the term is used in reference to currency, and usually currency that is not reported as income to the appropriate tax authority; but it might also be used in reference to your stolen car.)

The additional process involves taking the Alabama registration and plates to another state motor vehicle bureau to upgrade the quality of the registration. A favorite in this connection is New Jersey Motor Vehicle, for the simple reason that should you show up with only a registration (and no proof of ownership, such as a title) the state agency will accept your word as to ownership and provide you with a brand-new, and completely legal certificate of title. When I was in graduate school in New Jersey, I recall having done just that with my 1966 Triumph sports car. However, my car wasn't hot; I had bought it from a classmate. But the principle is exactly the same: the state agency had absolutely no way of knowing whether I was swearing to the truth.

An additional refinement may be added, if the ring is located in New York. With a spanking new title, registration and plates, compliments of the State of New Jersey, the car can then be registered yet again at New York Motor Vehicle. Then the New York plates are fastened onto the rear and front bumpers of the car, the registration signed over to the new owner, and the deal signed and delivered.

The overhead cost of these three registrations will run under one hundred dollars (the exact amount is a function of the actual weight of the vehicle). For another hundred, the car was stolen off the streets. Total overhead, for this method of operation, is three hundred dollars.

But this is not the most elegant procedure around. Basically, it is sloppy. Although the stolen and resold car has new plates and registration, it still retains the original vehicle identification number, the VIN. These VIN numbers, which run from six to ten digits long, are die-cast by the manufacturer to various pieces of metal on the car. (In newer models, they are usually on a separate metal plate at the top of the dashboard on the driver's side.) These VIN numbers are an additional aid to police identification of the vehicle. So, to play it completely safe, some rings will furnish the car with a new VIN number. They will either replace the plate, or erase two of the numbers and tap in, with a die tool, a new number or two that will alter the VIN number just enough.

(The less-professional organization will do the latter, since it is the cheapest method. Most policemen are not experienced enough in the field of auto theft to know the difference anyway, so that a quick touch-up of the VIN plate often suffices, even if the car is stopped on the road for a check.*)

More professional organizations go one step further. A friend of mine, who is an expert in the business, calls this method the Magic Wand Body Shop.

Magic Wand Body Shop will send a representative to a local salvage yard. He will walk up to the manager or owner and ask whether he has laying around a certain make and year car.

Say, he asks whether the yard has a junked 1973 Cadillac Eldorado. The owner of the junkyard says yes, there is one. The

* As virtually every criminal knows, there are additional "secret" VIN numbers imprinted on various other metallic parts of the automobile. The numbers appear on different parts of the car each year and are provided to police on a confidential basis. However, most criminals are informed about these "secret" locations by their contacts in both the automotive and police worlds, and most policemen ignore the hidden VIN numbers because they often have to take the car apart to get at them.

ring's man says, great, just what we've been looking for, how much? The yard owner says, for you, five hundred bucks.

Now, to the average person like you or me, five hundred dollars may seem like a lot for a pile of junk. But it's not, in this particular case.

For the ring's man is not buying the car. He's purchasing the VIN plates on the car, and the old registration.

When a junked car is brought in to a yard, the owner is supposed to turn over the old registration to the authorities. But some don't. The reason some don't is that an old registration on a junked car that is not hot is worth a lot of money.

Now the ring has in its possession a new VIN plate and an expired registration card for a non-hot car.

In turn, the ring orders a car from the street to fit the new documents. Word goes out for a 1973 Cadillac Eldorado. The next day just such a car is in the backyard of Magic Wand Body Shop, which magically converts the completely demolished Caddy in the junkyard into a beautiful, slightly used and very stolen automobile. The new owner of this car will now have a stolen car with non-stolen plates and a good registration. Unless police can detect the switched VIN plate (and few will be able to do so), the work of Magic Wand Body Shop will go undetected.

This method, of course, increases the overhead. The owner of the junkyard, who may know what the criminal is up to, may charge at least several hundred dollars for his cooperation. But the result is, as it were, a quality product. It is also a more professional way of doing business. When a buyer is a man known to the ring to be a professional criminal of some stature, for instance, this is the way it is done. For you or me, the average man on the street, though, the service may not be as thoughtful.

There are other aspects to the business which are also exceedingly lucrative to the professional criminal.

Cars stolen by small-scale operators—who, incidentally, tend to specialize in five-year-old Chevrolets within the price range of their clients,*—will not be thoroughly laundered. Instead, a car may be lifted off the street and provided only with forged registration papers. In many cities in the United States, basement printing shops grind out phony registration papers and even drivers' licenses that, in some cases, are of such quality that only an expertly trained police officer will be able to detect the forgery.

In yet another variation, the car thief may have a friend in a Motor Vehicle office who augments his or her income by providing, for ten dollars apiece, blank registration forms. These forms are then filled out as appropriate and validated with a dummy Motor Vehicle stamp.

Perhaps the most original variation on this theme is the so-called Avis fraud (or Hertz fraud). The criminal walks into a car rental office and rents a late-model car for one week. Then the criminal has his sister (or wife, or girl friend, or, perhaps, mother—especially popular among certain criminals) place an advertisement in the for-sale section of the local newspaper, offering the car at a real bargain price. In the meantime, the criminal obtains a phony registration document conforming to phony plates. Maybe the plates are simply transferred from the thief's own car, for, as we shall see, the time being.

Soon enough, the advertisement is answered. The price, after all, is right. The unsuspecting buyer goes to, say, the girl friend's house. There she is met by a distraught young woman, who tells her that her landlord is on the verge of throwing her out on the pavement unless the overdue rent is paid immediately. The customer is more than happy to assist the woman's cash-flow problem.

The buyer, for perhaps two thousand dollars, leaves in possession, she thinks, of an automobile worth at least three or four thousand. The buyer parks the car in front of her apartment. The

---

* Once my mechanic told me never to park my car in the Bronx. My car was a five-year-old Chevy with a 425-HP engine. He said it was a hot item. I didn't ask him how he knew. A year later, as the car started to fall apart, I contemplated driving it to the Bronx and leaving it overnight. After all, it was insured. But I didn't. Writer's conscience, perhaps?

next morning, she promises herself, she will take the registration and plates to Motor Vehicle to re-register the car in her own name.

That night the criminal walks up to the buyer's car, gets in behind the wheel, and drives away. How does he do this? He had made before turning the car over to his girl friend a duplicate set of keys precisely for the purpose of stealing the car anew.

In the papers the next day an ad for a late-model car appears. As it turned out, the girl friend had placed the ad to run for several days.

The fraud runs for a week. If seven sales are made, the fraud will net the criminal perhaps six thousand dollars or more. The overhead cost for the business will be the cost of the newspaper advertisements, the cost of the forged documents, and the cost of the weekly rental from Avis. For, at the very end of the Avis swindle, the criminal may actually return the car to Avis just like any other reliable rental customer. Incidentally, the criminal has probably rented the car under a phony registration, and paid for the car in advance with a cash deposit (thus obviating the need to show a credit card). Even if the police should perhaps uncover the perpetrator, they are unlikely to do it before the criminal and his girl friend make that plane to Caracas or the Riviera for a lavishly financed vacation.

No successful criminal enterprise of this nature can exist without a market. There is, of course, a demand for late-model cars at a discount price, and there are a great many people in the world who are not anxious to ask too many questions when presented with a tremendous bargain. The chapter on the fence illustrates this even more vividly. It is a theme that recurs in this book time and again.

In some sense of the term, auto theft is almost a victimless crime. New York policemen even call it a "happy crime." Like prostitution, gambling, and some forms of narcotics dealing, auto theft does not entail very dramatic violations of the citizen's rights. When a car is stolen, for instance, the victim does not wind up in the hospital and the criminal rarely winds up in jail. For all concerned there is very little trouble.

It is a happy crime, because the manufacturer of the stolen car is happy. He's happy to sell you a new car to replace the stolen one.

The salesman is happy. He's happy to get his second commission.

The insurance company people are happy. They are happy to pay you 80 percent of the value of the car and then go before the state insurance regulation agency next year and justify higher auto insurance premiums on the basis of the recent upsurge in car thefts.

And even the victim isn't in tears. At least he's got the insurance money. Maybe the car wasn't running that well anyway.

In fact, maybe he even asked for the car to be stolen. Or drove to a salvage dump and asked his good friend the proprietor to get rid of his gas-eating monster once and for all. And the proprietor will put the car through the shredder, take the registration and put it under the blotter, and wait for the ring's man to show up someday. And the owner calls the insurance company to report that his car has been stolen. He'll collect the insurance money and buy that low-gas-consumption Volkswagen that he should have purchased in the first place.

This happens every day. It is known as the insurance fraud, and it's just one of the ways American citizens get back at their insurance company (perhaps understandably, in view of rocketing premium costs)—in this instance with the eager participation of an underworld representative.

The one thing I've left out is the theft of motor vehicles not for the car itself but for the spare parts.

Put yourself in the place of a body-and-fender-shop owner. Your tow truck has just returned to your shop with a later model car on the hook. It had been hit in the front end with considerable damage to the two fenders, the grill and the hood. The owner says he is fully insured.

Maybe the next day the owner of the car comes back to your shop either to give you the contract for the job—or to pay the towing charges and take the car to another shop. Maybe the second shop said it could do the repair work in less time than you.

So now you are on the spot. You can play it straight and probably lose the job, or you can play it crooked and make a bundle.

If you play it straight you tell the customer, "Well, you need a nose clip. Two fenders, the grill, the hood, lights and wires. I'll have to order from the manufacturer and if you are lucky and he has it in stock it'll take a few days. It will come back to me in pieces, and must be put together. Then, after I put it on the car, I have to paint it to match your car and then install the wires and lights. This will take at least a week, maybe two."

So you risk having the customer run out on you.

Choice two: You play it crooked, according to the American way of crime. If you choose this direction, you will be able to say, "It will be ready in a day or two." And you might also say, "The estimate will be $1,600, but I'll give you back one hundred dollars from your insurance check." This, as one of my good, cynical friends in the New York Police Department puts it, makes for a "guaranteed sale."

Now all you have to do is to call your favorite thief, or car-ring contact, and tell him you need a nose clip for a certain make, certain year, certain color. By the next morning you've got the part, he's got a hundred dollars of your money, you've got fifteen hundred dollars of the insurance company's money, and the customer has a repaired front end and a hundred dollars in cash to go to the track with. By doing this you will have increased your profit enormously at approximately zero risk; few parts of any auto are stamped with identifiable serial numbers.

One parts thief I know said this: "I think stealing parts is even bigger than stealing for the whole car. Even when the big boys get a hold of a complete car, they strip it for parts, or maybe put the parts of one car on another to change the identity. Parts theft is where the dough is."

One of the real ironies of the car-theft business concerns the role of the insurance company. Although all insurance companies employ trained investigators, they are not equipped to conduct thorough investigations on most cases, and as a general rule are no match for the professionally run car-theft and spare-parts business. As a result, according to a study of car thefts in Canada and the United States conducted by the Royal Canadian Mounted Police, in many cases the same insurance company that paid for the repair of a particular car also had to pay out for the theft of the vehicle that was stolen for the parts for the repair of the first vehicle. (This is because the insurance company pays for all new parts and almost never checks to determine that only *new* parts are used.)

In the American way of crime, criminals work with low overhead and high profits. This is the only way they work.

Stealing cars is a very good business for them. The overhead is ridiculously low, and the profit level the envy of legitimate used-car outfits. Besides, any good crime, in the American way of crime, requires the cooperation of the average American man on the street. Without the so-called legitimate businessman and citizen on board, the business would be infinitely more risky—and, worse still, less profitable.

Who can resist a late-model car at a "real steal"?

Who can turn down a cheap—and "fast"—repair job, even if the circumstances are somewhat mysterious.

CHAPTER THREE

Seed Money

MANY VIOLENT crimes in America are committed out of frustration, inexperience and, most certainly, madness. However, many are committed out of a purely rational desire to put together a stake for reinvestment in a racket. Currently the narcotics racket is the most common recipient of seed money, and bank robbery is one of the most common vehicles for getting it.

A young man from Brooklyn is now serving time in a federal prison for bank robbery. Sometime in the winter and spring of 1972–1973, he had decided to rob commercial banks and savings institutions. His targets included some of the most prestigious banks in the United States, including the Chase Manhattan banks. At first, it was thought that this young man was embarking on the classic seed-money-crime pattern. Then something happened that changed everyone's mind.

Seed money is the money the burgeoning criminal gets from his first big score. With this in hand, the young entrepreneur feels he holds the key to the future, can dream of moving into another area of crime, perhaps attracting the favorable attention of a better-connected criminal.

The need for seed money is probably responsible for a major percentage of the visible crimes in the United States. Visible crimes —the bank robberies, muggings, supermarket holdups, and so forth—are not the exclusive province of young men on the way up, but they are largely so. The young initiate commits a very high percentage of the visible and often violent crimes, precisely because he doesn't know what else to do and hasn't anything else to do. What he does is not professional crime; it is on the fringe. Violent, visible crime and professional crime are almost direct opposites. The whole point of professional crime is for the public not to see the violence, not to realize that they are being held up, in one way or another. The inevitable excesses of youthful criminals are antithetical to this idea, for the acquisition of seed money is often absurdly horrific. At the same time, it is not senseless crime. It makes sense to the perpetrator to acquire seed money.

The young man from Brooklyn was black, stood six feet five inches tall, and weighed two hundred pounds. He was well-built, quiet, and from all appearances, not dumb by any means.

His method of operation was superficially professional: the note-job technique. This is the method used by many professional bank robbers today. The robber, often but not necessarily working alone, walks into a bank and places a threatening note under the eyes of a teller. He does not point a loaded carbine at people or fire shots into the air. The message is contained in the threat of violence rather than its actual manifestation.

It is a successful technique, for everyone is well aware that bank officials instruct their tellers to cooperate fully with bank robbers at every turn. It is axiomatic that whereas money can be replaced, human life cannot. Indeed, bank deposits, like most American automobiles, are fully insured for theft.

The young man seemed, at first, exceptionally well suited to the patient operation of the note job. For example, on March 12, 1973, he strolled into a branch of Chemical Bank in Manhattan like any other customer. It was noon, and the bank floor was mobbed with depositors. He walked directly to a deposit table; he was wearing a wide brown hat, brown trench coat, and dark leather shoes. In this

particular bank the man hardly drew a second glance; the branch
was located in Harlem, and most of the other customers were black
as well. In this, the criminal was, perhaps not intentionally, shrewd.
A black man, especially one six feet five, would stand out in a bank
patronized largely by whites as a white criminal would in a black-
patronized establishment.

Like many other persons in this bank, the criminal used a bank
form to indicate a withdrawal, but he filled it out differently. On the
back of the ticket was written in bold blue letters:

PUT ALL THE MONEY IN THE BAG. DON'T SOUND ANY ALARM
OR YOU WILL BE SHOT IN YOUR FACE. MY MAN AT THE DOOR
ALSO HAS A GUN AIMED AT YOUR HEAD.

The robber stood patiently in line like all the other customers.
When his turn in front of the teller came, he calmly shoved the note
under the bars. Just as calmly, the teller filled up his brown-paper
bag with hundred-dollar bills. When he left the bank for his
scamper down crowded Amsterdam Avenue, his brown bag held
$5,000.

On the whole, a smart crime all the way around. The teller is
left after the ordeal with his life and limb intact, the bank is left
with filling out federal-insurance papers for reimbursement from
government for the stolen money, and the criminal escaped from
the scene of the crime without so much as a single hair mussed up.

This man pulled many other bank robberies using no more than
a threatening note. In fact, in each and every robbery the language
of the note was identical. On March 21, 1973, he robbed the
Chemical branch at 103 East 125th Street of $2,586; on March
30, Chemical, at 3205 Broadway, for $1,370; on April 2, an insti-
tution known as the Empire Savings Bank, at 3377 Broadway, for
$2,824.

It is to be noted that in each of these robberies no one was hurt,
the robbery was efficient, quick, and he made his getaway by
simply thrusting himself into the street crowd outside the bank.
Police later summoned to the scene of the crime had no more to go

on than a general description of a tall, male black wearing a brown hat. Although each of these banks was equipped with security television monitors, the robber didn't even bother to wear a mask. Even though the police were thereby provided with an instant replay of each criminal event, the videotape was of little use in locating the criminal, since he was not a well-known figure. Besides, cameras don't start, on most security systems, until switched on by alarm button.

Then one day he made a blunder. He used force and escalated his crime from simple robbery to assault on a person. This more than anything else drew heightened attention from police.

On April 9, 1973, he entered a nice, gleaming-new Chase Manhattan Bank branch at 2218 Fifth Avenue. The bank is a one-story glass-and-concrete structure on the southwest corner of 135th Street and Fifth Avenue, in the heart of Harlem.

He entered the bank through the revolving door on Fifth Avenue and strode directly toward a customer table, as usual. To his back, on the right as one enters this bank, is the teller counter. To the very rear of the bank is the vault area, where considerable sums of money are stored. But he wasn't interested in carting away huge piles of money. His method of operation was cash-and-carry; the second man to whom his threatening notes alluded was a non-existent personage.

On this day, for some unknown reason, he was impatient about waiting on line like any other customer. In fact, he didn't. Pushing past the persons ahead of him in the line, he had made quite a commotion by the time he got to the teller's cage.

This was mistake number one. For in making a scene he alerted another teller at a different cage to the possibility of imminent foul play.

Undaunted—indeed, unaware that an alarm had even been activated—he shoved the note to the teller and said menacingly, "Fill it up, fill it up."

The teller at Window 5, wisely disdaining the role of the hero, calmly filled up his white canvas bag with several thousand dollars in cash. Outside, a security guard at Daitch-Shopwell, a grocery supermarket across the street, happened to be staring at the bank.

To the criminal, the teller appeared slow in filling the bag. "Hurry up, hurry up," he shouted, perspiration forming on his brow.

As the teller was nodding assent, the bank guard did a dumb thing. He drew his gun.

The criminal turned from Window 5 with his satchel of cash in hand. Then he saw the guard with the gun. The guard was too pulverized with fear to do anything but wave his gun. The criminal by this time had his handgun drawn, aimed at the guard's chest, and fired once.

Across the street the observant supermarket security man heard a shot, saw the guard fall to the ground, saw a six-foot man race out of the Fifth Avenue entrance of the bank, and saw the bank robber disappear into the midday crowd swarming along Fifth Avenue.

Back in the bank people gasped, the guard lay moaning with a .22-caliber bullet in his chest, and bank officials phoned for the police.

By the time the nearest patrol car reached the scene of the crime, the robber from Brooklyn was presumably miles from the bank. The police rushed the wounded guard to the hospital (he recovered), took down eyewitness accounts, and called in agents from the Federal Bureau of Investigation's bank-robbery unit (all bank robberies are federal offenses, hence FBI involvement).

Even with this telling lack of judgment, the criminal might never have been apprehended. Despite videotape television cameras in banks, bank robbery remains a relatively easy score (which is one reason why many amateurs and political radicals go into it; another reason is that when they decide to rob a bank, they at least are secure in the knowledge that if all goes well they will exit with cash, rather than with merchandise that would require the services of a perhaps kiss-and-tell fence to convert into cash).

However, two weeks later this criminal was arrested. He had

been sighted by a local merchant in the vicinity of the very bank he had robbed. The merchant recognized him from an FBI photograph from the videotape machine, and contacted police. Under questioning, the criminal admitted his motive: he had robbed the banks not for seed money, but to supply himself with heroin. The criminal was an addict.

It is probably safe to assume that, had our robber been thinking of a career rather than a fix, he'd be on the streets today, for his mode of operation was professional. Only his motive was not. No wonder he was caught (and was stupid enough to roam in the vicinity of a recent operation); he was, after all, an addict, and addicts tend not to make *professional* criminals. It is a generalization that every day is confirmed and reconfirmed by arrest figures, which everywhere in the country show that an enormous percentage of addict-criminals have arrest records as long as their well-punctured arms.

Another youth went about the rookie business of seed money in a different way. He tried "scientific" mugging. In 1972 and the winter of 1973, an 18-year-old high school graduate who lived in Manhattan went on a mugging spree. But he exhibited somewhat more imagination than hundreds of young hoodlums in New York.

During this period the young criminal committed twenty-eight separate muggings. But they were not committed on a random basis. After each mugging, the young man went back to his room, took out a loose-leaf book in his desk drawer, and wrote down several pieces of information, in this precise order:

> Date of the act
> Place
> Exact time of day
> Sex of the victim
> Color (and sometimes the race) of the victim
> Exact amount of the take

Weapon used to obtain the victim's compliance
Additional items (clothing, valuables, etc.) taken
Whether the victim was an "E," or a "Y," or a "C" (for
"Elderly," "Young," or "Child")
Whether the incident was an "R" (that is, the victim put up
some resistance)

Why did he compile such information? There are several theories. Police who later interviewed the young man thought, simply enough, that he was just a very bright entrepreneur who kept notes on his activities the way a young musician might write down his practice hours daily.

But possibly he simply wanted to find the most efficient way in which to carry on the business of mugging. He wanted to know such things as (1) what was the best time of day to mug in terms of safety for himself and amount of take; (2) where was the best place in the city; (3) was it in the long run worth taking anything other than the victim's cash and change?

Judging from the diary, this young mugger must have come to these conclusions:

First, the best time of day was anytime of day, but usually around noon. His last group of entries showed these times: 11:25 A.M., 11:45 A.M., 11:55 A.M., and 12:22 P.M. This flies in the face of the conventional theories about mugging, which is that late afternoon and early evening are the best times, since this is when most people are coming home from work and are tired, unwary and willing to surrender.

His second major conclusion—as to the best place—appeared to be in a section of the Bronx, and in particular a section populated largely by aging men and women who, as it turned out, were Jewish. It seemed he believed that these persons would be easiest to mug.

Third, toward the end of this mugger's diary, every one of his victims was female, white, and elderly.

Fourth, toward the end of his diary, the mugger almost always took not only money from the victim but also some other article, whether the purse itself, an article of clothing (such as a hat), or even several items from the shopping bag. Looking back at the mugger's experience, it was easy to see why. As I interpret the figures in his diary, which is now in the possession of the New York Police Department (it's something of a collector's item), the eighteen-year-old criminal took in a grand total of $260.13 over a five-month stretch. This averages out to a mere $6.78 a hit, hardly a gold mine for an ambitious entrepreneur.

Eventually, the young mugger was picked up by police in the act of assaulting an eighty-year-old woman. It turned out that as he began concentrating on one particular stretch of the city because it was the easiest to do and the most lucrative, the police began concentrating there too—precisely because muggings seemed to occur in this one stretch of New York with unusual frequency. Little did they know, until they saw this unusual diary, that the area was being worked repeatedly by an amateur cost accountant.

The mugger was caught early. He learned the lesson the hard way. The lesson is that mugging is a very tough way to get together a stake. The criminal has to assault feloniously too many people. And if the motive is to get money for the personal use of drugs, the job becomes even tougher. The addict can never get enough money for drugs, and a lot of money is precisely what the mugging business does not offer in abundance. To be sure, occasionally the mugger might be lucky, stumbling across a dumb pedestrian who just cashed a winning lottery ticket at the local bank. But in an age wherein credit cards have replaced cash, and checks are readily accepted for merchandise, most people do not walk the streets with a great deal of cash on them. For this reason alone, mugging now seems, to most criminals I talk to, a losing enterprise.

But there is another reason for its unpopularity among serious-minded criminals bent on getting ahead. They know—or at least the smart ones do—that any act of violence increases the chances of having to do time. Police would rather arrest a robbery suspect than a burglar, no matter what the relative dollar amounts might be. When a young man runs around with a thirteen-inch butcher knife held to the throats of defenseless elderly people, and from each of these flirtations with murder or manslaughter gets away with but a few dollars, then this young criminal is going against the grain of professional American crime. Ultimately muggers are caught; rarely do they get ahead; almost inevitably they fail at the business of crime.

A young criminal in search of seed money apparently has to rely on his own devices—unless he is quite lucky. This would involve being noticed by a burglary ring or by some organized crime outfit in the market for some new blood. Then, the young criminal would receive assignments from the organization and be paid accordingly —usually on a per-job basis, but sometimes on a retainer plus a percentage.

A young man who was born and raised in San Francisco once told me how he used to get up enough money to buy narcotics. He didn't use dope himself, just retailed the stuff to addicts. This young man spent several years along the East Coast as a hotel burglar.

His method of operation was simplicity itself. One time in Philadelphia he looked up a friend from the West Coast, who was working part-time as a night clerk at a Philadelphia hotel. The hotel was not a luxury-class establishment, but it was a respected place, took all credit cards, gave clean linen daily, and so forth. In addition, it was located downtown and in that locale attracted considerable convention trade.

This young criminal, as professionally minded about his work as the average law-school graduate, always looked forward to conventions. It was not that he himself derived pleasure from contact with the conventioneers. It was just that he profited from grown men getting plastered until the wee hours of the morning, abandoning their hotel rooms for hours at a time.

This youth called his friend at the hotel. He asked him whether he could use seventy-five dollars. His friend, who studied during the day at a local technical institute, was quick to say yes.

When this young man registered at this hotel, he was given two keys by the desk clerk. The first was a key to *his* room, the second was a master key to most of the other rooms in that hotel. Upon reaching his room, our man took some key-cutting equipment out of his attaché case and made a copy of the master key the desk clerk had so thoughtfully given him. Then he went back downstairs and slid an envelope across the front desk to his friend. The envelope contained the master key and seventy-five dollars.

By this time, as the man recalls this typical burglary, it was about eight in the evening. Still too early to go to work; the conventioneers had barely finished dinner.

The burglar picked up the telephone to get the hotel operator. This move was a standard part of the operation. When she answered, he told the woman to wake him up at six o'clock, saying he had to catch an early flight out of town. "Six," says the operator, "Room 234 at six. Goodnight, sir."

Then he set his own portable night-table alarm clock for 2 A.M., and dozed off to sleep. When the alarm went off, the young man, refreshed from his nap, was ready for work.

At this time of the morning it's easy to tell who's in his room and who's not. Usually, during a convention, a great many of the delegates are out at some night spot, or downstairs at the hotel bars and lounges. As a general rule the young criminal holds that at two in the morning in the middle of a convention very few delegates are in their rooms sleeping. And even if they are, he insists, they are completely bombed. In the event our criminal should enter an occupied room, chances are the smashed delegate would never notice.

It takes an expert hotel burglar at most two hours to go through a dozen rooms. This young criminal was very thorough. Using the copy of the master key, he entered each room and searched the luggage first, looking for hidden money, other valuables, possibly traveler's checks (which he can fence at a travel agency downtown).

Then he rifled the pockets of all clothing in the room, looking for forgotten spare change, maybe a watch or a ring, possibly spare credit cards. Then he checked all the drawers as well as the most common hiding places for valuables. Under the pillow, under the mattress, under the telephone, taped under lamp shades—places like that.

As a general rule the burglar will not enter a hotel room near an elevator. He prefers rooms farther down the corridor. In this way he can hear anyone coming up or down that hall. If he's too close to the elevator, the occupant can be out the elevator door and fumbling for his keys before he had a chance to either escape or hide. The great advantage of working conventions, however, is that the occupant of the room upon getting out of the elevator will likely be singing in an inebriated forte voice. In the setting of a convention the victim serves as an early-warning system for the criminal.

Once this young burglar was caught inside a room as a drunken conventioneer thundered in, dropped off his clothes, and flopped like a fallen tree into bed. As he fell, he barely missed our young man, who was crouching by the side of the bed. The conventioneer missed him by a fraction of an inch. The criminal was assisted in his escape from the room by the fact that convention-going men who have been drinking rarely turn the lights on before retiring, or so my source suggests. This one didn't.

It was then 5:45 in the morning. The burglar gets back to his room just as his phone is ringing. It's the operator with his 6 A.M. wake-up call. Trying for all the world to sound drowsy and beat, the criminal thanks the operator, goes into the bathroom to throw some water on his face, and heads downstairs.

The conventioneers are sleeping so soundly the snores can be heard through the oak doors.

As he goes past the front desk he waves goodbye to the desk clerk, drops off his room key, and doesn't even have to stop to pay his bill. The reason he doesn't stop is that he has paid his bill the night before. In five minutes he is in the downtown Greyhound

Bus Station and hops the first bus out of town. By the time the conventioneers awake, the thief is long gone.

The young criminal says there is only one thing wrong with working hotels in Philadelphia. He complains that the town is so dead at night, conventioneers often have nowhere to go to get drunk except their hotel rooms. He says that he once worked a hotel and there were only a half dozen or so rooms unoccupied by delegates creating their own night life. Such limitations do not hamper his work at hotels in New York, San Francisco and Miami.

Headed out of town, the burglar is sitting in the back of the bus by himself, counting the take. He has more than $500 in cash, perhaps another $700 in jewelry and watches. The traveler's checks he has already put in a special-delivery envelope addressed to his friend the fence at a local travel agency. By the time American Express has distributed the hot numbers, his friend will have fenced the checks. The young criminal will get 25 percent of the take. On the bus he figures this will come to another $250. He'll collect it on his next trip to town.

His take adds up to roughly $1,500.

His overhead was $95 (not counting the bus ticket)—$20 for the room rental, $75 for the desk clerk.

With $1,400 this young man can buy a very good ounce of heroin or several sets of very fine burglar tools.

It's at least a start. Seed money.

CHAPTER FOUR

He Can Get It for You Less Than Wholesale

HE STANDS behind the neighborhood bar or sits in the back of the little dress store downtown or is the owner pumping gas at the corner gas station. He is the fence, the professional connection between the underworld and the surface world, and in some ways the buffer zone between them.

The fence conveys the thief's stolen goods beyond the reach of the long arms of the law and into the hands of the more or less— and usually *less*—legitimate businessmen. He sells the merchandise to the businessman at a price less than the businessman can obtain elsewhere, and returns to the thief a percentage of the take in a shorter period of time than the thief could unload the goods. The fence's role is to serve two different masters; the key to his success is that he comes out on top of them both.

He is the underworld's indispensable man. The businessman can purchase the hot goods without ever having to confront on a face-to-face basis the thief or hijacker; and the thief never has to expose himself to the businessman, who in the event of a police investigation might be the first to break down.

The good fence is a man of a thousand connections. He will know many professional burglars and boosters (department store thieves) in his area, and he may know more about the business of stealing than the thieves themselves; and he is perhaps wiser in the ways of the so-called legitimate businessmen (a term used in this book with a not unwarranted amount of sarcasm) than the Better Business Bureau. He will have a working relationship with any number of boosters, burglars, hijackers, and other fences, as well as contacts in the straight world with whom he regularly conducts business. In fact, as suggested above, the fence may be the owner of a legitimate business and conduct absolutely legal commerce with other businesses even as he disposes of stolen merchandise to these same businesses under the counter.

All fences are not alike. Some are friendly father figures whose clients come to them with a variety of requests, such as bail money, advice on their love life or anything under the sun; and others are absolute sharks whom you wouldn't ask for a dollar, a donation to the Girl Scouts or the time of day. Moreover, some fences are generalists who will dispose of everything from baby diapers to Sterno sets. Others are specialists, confining their trade to such exotic items as jewelry, art objects, cameras, and the like.

All working fences are careful folk. They tend to dress like conservative businessmen and keep as low a profile as possible. They go quietly about their business, which is to become a millionaire as rapidly as possible, in anticipation of eventual retirement and residence in that condominium by the sea. They are the steadiest, least violence-prone members of the profession, and they have a reputation for keeping their word in business deals. They are, in the strange way of the underworld, the businessman's businessman.

As a white-collar traffic manager in what is essentially a blue- and gray-collar world, the fence can command considerable respect and influence. To the young burglar, the fence can prove a kind of seminar teacher who may frequently lecture on the ins and outs of the profession (and sometimes even give specific advice, like where and when to hit a truck or a store or an apartment). To the hard-core truck hijacker, who usually is connected with organized crime, the fence is the instant outlet, a professional whose word is gold; when the fence says he can handle a load, as a friend of mine once put it, *"he can handle a load."* This is important to a hijacker, who after all would have only limited personal use for, say, four thousand Hitachi radios.

To the organized-crime executive, the high-volume fence, like himself, is a businessman of the black market. He is also, in the world of hot-blooded young thieves and pistol-packing hijackers, a source of reassurance that someone else out there has a head on his shoulders. In fact, to just about all concerned, the fence is living proof that in the business of crime, professionalism really pays.

Spider's* general store is located a few blocks from Independence Hall in downtown Philadelphia. Whenever I am in Philadelphia, I drop in to see what's hot. I rarely buy, just like to look. But Spider's is not your average general store.

Spider's is owned by a man with wide connections in the world of crime. He is one of the more active fences of general merchandise on the East Coast. He may not be the biggest fence around, but he is one of the least discriminate. He'll take almost anything, as a casual perusal of his store demonstrates.

From the outside, his place is not much to look at. It has a green awning, is about twenty feet wide, and displays all sorts of merchandise in windows that have not been cleaned too recently. Spider's could use a good exterior paint job, but actually it doesn't make much difference. People don't come to Spider's for the atmosphere. They come for the values.

Most of the stuff Spider handles comes from professional thieves and hijackers. And some of it goes to so-called legitimate businessmen elsewhere in the city and the East. But a certain portion of it winds up on the shelves and glass counters of his own store. When-

* Spider's is not the store's real name. I might get my hands rapped if I told you the correct name. But everything else in this account is accurate to the letter.

ever I am in Spider's, it is always pretty crowded. I don't know whether they come to buy, or only to get a glimpse of Spider, who in certain circles is considered the genuine article.

Let me give you a quick idea of the vast array of Spider's merchandise. Some of it is pure junk. Dolls, toy racing cars, plastic animals, doll houses, dart games, potholders, spray paint, and the like. On the other hand, some of it is pretty good stuff. For some reason, which I have never been able to determine, in Spider's there is a vaster collection of Old Spice, Brut, Fabergé and other male toilet articles than I have seen in most drugstores. Maybe he deals with criminals who like to smell nice, as a regular patron once put it. In any event, there is, besides, all sorts of ladies' perfumes and powders, lots of pantyhose and stockings, occasional hats and scarfs, and costume jewelry of all descriptions. In the back, hanging on regular clothing racks, are men's suits of considerable quality, raincoats, and the like.

Not all of this stuff is hot, in fact. A lot of the items are closeouts, seconds, last year's fashions which Spider got on the cheap. But much of the stuff is as hot as a tamale. By mixing together the hot and the cool he gives the impression that *everything* is hot at Spider's, a clever device which, as you might imagine, tends to stimulate buying considerably.

Inside the store on this rainy July day Spider is showing a customer a new suit of clothes. Most of his clothing comes from professional thieves who sell their loot to him at between 15 and 25 percent of the catalogue wholesale value. In turn, Spider sells the clothing either to a retail store at 80 to 90 percent of list wholesale price, or in his store at up to 75 percent of retail. Either way, Spider profits. Spider never pays the thief more than one third of wholesale for the stolen goods, so that, if you figure it out, if the listed wholesale price of an item is ten dollars, Spider will pay the thief maybe three dollars, fence it to a clothing store for nine dollars (to be sold to you off the rack at slightly less than retail), and pocket the six dollars as profit.

One day I was in Philadelphia to attend the sentencing of Stanley

Wolfe, a fence whom you will soon meet. The day before the sentencing, after checking into a hotel, I dropped by Spider's. I needed a wind-up traveling alarm clock.

One of Spider's young assistants said he had just the thing. It was a fully guaranteed, wind-up clock, he said. It was even decorated with a basketball on top as the alarm bells. The only thing was, he said, it had the official team insignia of the "Seattle Supersonics" emblazoned across the clock's face.

"Got many Seattle fans in Philly?" I asked.

Spider spoke up from the back. Spider is a short, quite rotund man who seems always to wear short-sleeved shirts open at the collar. He said: "Do you want it or not?"

"I want it, but do I have to pay sticker price?"

The sticker price was $11.95. Actually, it was a pretty good wind-up clock. Sturdy, colorful. And, if you were a Seattle fan, it was a *terrific* clock.

Spider said, "For you, five dollars."

I whipped out my wallet and gave his assistant *exactly* five dollars. (The fence does not collect city sales tax.) I now have a Seattle Supersonic alarm clock in the bedroom of my Manhattan apartment. It is, one might say, a conversation piece.

Just then, a loud horn blared outside. Spider eyed one of his customers suspiciously. He was concerned that no one violated the parking laws in front of his store.

"You double-parked?" he barked.

"Not me, honest," said the customer. "I'm parked legit." Spider was relieved; like many criminals, he seeks to establish superficially correct relations with law enforcement.

Back at the hot-suit rack, Spider was working his usual silken charm on a customer in the market for a pair of slacks.

The customer said he'd take a pair of size-36. Spider showed him a nice pair of green slacks that looked to be worth thirty dollars. How much, the customer asked. "For you," said Spider, "fifteen dollars."

"I'll take 'em," said the customer.

"Don't you want to try them on?" said Spider.

"Nah, why should I? Even if they don't fit, I can always sell them myself for thirty dollars!"

Everyone in the fence's store laughed.

There is no mystery about the fence's success. He is an integral part of a competitive economy. The fence is the man who can get it for you less than wholesale.

In a competitive market, buyers are attracted to lower prices like water to its own level. Precisely because the fence buys lower than anyone else, he can sell lower than anyone else. (If the average fence advertised in the newspaper, there'd be a line twice around his block every day.) Because the fence undersells the competition, he is a threat to legitimate business, and the fence's operation becomes a priority matter for the authorities. One such fence was Stanley Wolfe. With his brother Nathan, he ran a high-volume clothing-fence operation on the East Coast.

Nathan and Stanley Wolfe were Philadelphia boys. At some unknown point in their careers, they began trafficking in the interstate transportation of stolen merchandise. At the time of their apprehension by the FBI, they were running a million-dollar-a-year-volume business.

The professional fence will often rent a store front for a month or two and then move on to a new location to avoid suspicion. Between 1969 and 1972, Stanley and Nathan Wolfe rented some twenty-two different store-front establishments. And Stanley armed himself with more than a dozen aliases—names like Stanley Capit, Robert Kravitz, Silbey Wolfe, to mention just a few. One thing that Stanley was not, as investigators were to come to understand, was imprudent.

Stanley was also a quite distinguished-looking gentleman. He dressed conservatively, but smart. He often carried a cane, probably to cushion the pain from his arthritis, and wore silver-rimmed spectacles. He stood about five feet nine inches tall, weighed one hundred and seventy-five pounds, and had a well-chiseled nose that gave him an almost patrician bearing. In no way did Stanley Wolfe look like a thug.

Nathan, his brother, was stouter and less dapper. And, according to investigators who knew him, he wasn't as shrewd as his brother, either. "Stanley was the mastermind of the operation," said one federal agent.

In many respects Stanley was a classic fence. As he became more and more specialized in the area of women's and children's clothing, he became as knowledgeable about the intricacies of the garment industry as a garment center insider (in fact, his father had been a New York garment center worker). Most fences know as much about their particular line of business as the legitimate businessman.

Stanley was also pretty good at juggling money. One of the classic tricks he practiced was the double endorsement. This is how it works:

The Problem: A fence always tries to look like a legitimate businessman, even if he's always moving from one store to the next. (Even the Spider handled cold as well as hot items.) One key, in the business world, to appearing legitimate is to show a record for all financial transactions. If you are a shipper, you have the receiver (a generic and legal term for the purchaser of stolen goods) sign a receipt; if you are a trucker, you have a bill of lading; if you are a receiver you have the trucker sign a receipt. So what do you do if your "trucker" is a hijacker of stolen goods?

The Solution: The hijacker comes to the fence with the goods. He and the fence dicker on the price. Agreement is reached. The hijacker, of course, has no stationery to present as a receipt; he does not want to be identified with the goods. The fence, however, has a different problem, and he works it out by making out a check from Bank Account A for a certain amount. Usually this amount represents the approximate wholesale price of the merchandise to be fenced. Of course, the hijacker received significantly less than the actual wholesale price from the fence, and was paid off in cash. But the charade continues. The fence makes out this check to the burglar, using a fictitious name. I know one fence who used to sign it over to a Mr. Howdy Doody, so great was his contempt for the civilities of the banking business. Then the burglar endorsed his "Mr. Doody" back to the fence.

The next day the fence takes the endorsed check—the hijacker has signed his phony name on the back, remember—and adds to it his own, real name. This is the double endorsement. The fence then deposits this check, drawn on Bank Account A, into Bank Account B. Should an investigator claim that a certain load of goods in the fence's possession is stolen, the fence at least has the line of defense of saying that so-and-so "came into my store, offered me the goods, I paid him by check at actual wholesale value, and would have let it go at that except the seller needed the money right away; so I took the check to my bank [Bank B] and cashed it for him." The fence will use the double endorsement as proof of legitimate sale. "How was I to know," argues the fence, "that the stuff was hot? As you can see by the price I paid, I hardly got a very good deal."

The double-endorsement trick will not fool a sharp law-enforcement official. But it has baffled juries, at least to the point of acquittal. By the way, this procedure not only serves to help protect the fence; it also protects the thief, since investigators do not learn a great deal from the phony endorsement.

(A sharp bank will immediately put a stop to this practice, however. In fact, the Bank and Trust Company of Philadelphia—Stanley's bank—bluntly informed him that it would no longer accept for deposit checks drawn on his name, endorsed by the payee, and then re-endorsed by the payer. Most fences will open and close accounts before the banks get wind of what's going on.)

Another typical fence trick, practiced to perfection by Stanley Wolfe, was to orchestrate hijackings. Once Stanley telephoned a receiver to inquire whether a certain load of goods might prove interesting. Wolfe explained that a contact of his knew of a truck driver who, for ten thousand dollars, "will sleep for six hours," as

Stanley, in the parlance of the trade, put it. Actually, the truck driver was probably prepared to sleep for a great deal less than ten thousand—the difference being Stanley's finder's fee.

By 1972 Stanley and Nathan had settled themselves into a small, dumpy store at 3226 N. Cheltenham Avenue, in northwest Philadelphia, a store about 15 feet wide and 40 feet deep. It had two floors. On the top floor was the office, a tiny cubicle with a pair of telephones and a naked light bulb hanging overhead. At all times both this floor and the one below held vast quantities of merchandise. The Wolfe inventory consisted almost solely of female clothing. British Mist, Jonathan Logan, Bleecker Street, Talia Fashions, Excello, Laureno, Shawn, Sears, Thayer (Italy) were just a few of the reputable name brands on the racks of the Cheltenham Avenue store known to the receivers as Cedarbrook Fashions.

The store was located in a modest exurban shopping center. To the right was a respectable loan company; to the left a dry cleaner's. A few doors to the left of the dry cleaner's was a dark, cavernous bar where Stanley occasionally drank with a client to nail down a deal.

Half a mile away was an apartment complex known as Cedarbrook Apartments. Perhaps the name of the complex was the inspiration for the name of the firm. In the middle of the three towers in the complex, on the top floor, was Stanley Wolfe's penthouse apartment.

He commuted between his penthouse and his shabby office in a late-model Lincoln Continental. A lady who worked as a clerk at the cleaners said Stanley usually worked an 11-A.M.-to-4-P.M. shift, two or three days a week. A neighbor and resident at the Cedarbrook Apartment complex told investigators that Stanley was forever bragging about his hidden bank accounts in the Bahamas and Florida.

Between 1972 and 1974 Stanley and Nathan put together an awesome fencing operation that was the talk of the East Coast underworld. What everyone is still talking about is not so much the volume involved, though it was considerable, but the fact of its remarkable specialization—by this time the Wolfes had refined their operation to the fencing of women's and children's clothing.

Between October 1972 and February 1973, a period for which figures are most accurate, a quarter of a million dollars in such merchandise was fenced. And the operation was simplicity itself.

The major elements in the operation were:

1. An employee of a major wholesaler in the heart of the garment district of New York was in on the operation. The firm he worked for was called Volume Merchandise Inc., a national outfit which managed more than seventeen discount stores around the country and handled an annual sales gross of some one hundred million dollars.

2. A pair of small trucking firms were in on the deal. The trucking firms were located in Oceanside, Long Island, New York, and together amounted to a half dozen or so regular trucks, a handful of trailers, and three or so tractors. At the time of this writing, the trucking firms were still under investigation.

3. A small-time middleman who served as the communications hub and buffer element among the various parties; his name was Mario Stracuzza. At the time he was employed by a third trucking firm, which was not involved. Stracuzza fit into the picture because he knew Simone, the wholesaler employee, and the Wolfes had put the two together.

4. Stanley and Nathan themselves, who provided the initial cash outlay and the continuing interest in the operation; they served as fences of goods siphoned off by Simone.

5. Legitimate businesses across the United States; these were primarily small clothing stores and chain discount houses. I won't mention their names in this book; the number of so-called legitimate businesses who willingly, even happily deal with fences and other shady operators is probably a staggering figure, but they are very much an integral part of the profession's business.

The team worked like this:

Early every morning Nick Simone, the floor manager, prepared for the transfer of a considerable quantity of clothing from the warehouse of Volume Merchandise, located on the Lower West Side of New York, to various trucking carriers. In the midst of this massive movement of goods from shipping floor to truck, Nick Simone managed to sequester a small amount of stuff specially earmarked for one of the two trucking firms. Usually the truck arrived and was loaded with this special merchandise an hour or so before the arrival of the other trucks. Then Simone supervised the loading of the rest of the merchandise, some of which was added onto the truck already carrying the contraband.

The driver of the truck was provided with bills of lading for the legitimately loaded stuff, as well as some blank forms to be used later by the Wolfes.

The driver then headed directly for the home office in Oceanside. There, in the parking lot of the firm, the special shipment was unloaded onto an idle trailer and left there until a representative of the Wolfe operation appeared.

In the meantime, Simone informed Stracuzza of the most recent move. Stracuzza then called the Wolfes at Cedarbrook Fashions in Philadelphia. This is how one call went—word for word—on the morning of February 21, 1973 (Stracuzza, incidentally, calls here collect!):*

STRACUZZA: "Hello?"
NATHAN: "Yeah?"
STRACUZZA: "Tomorrow."
NATHAN: "Tomorrow, definitely?"
STRACUZZA: "Yeah."
NATHAN: "Ocean?"
STRACUZZA: "Yes."

This typically laconic exchange was the signal for the Wolfes to dispatch a driver, usually a part-time college student who may or may not have known the true score, to the Oceanside parking lot. Most times the driver was a student at Temple University (which,

---

* Their phone was wiretapped by federal agents, with court authorization. I have edited these intercepted conversations slightly for sense.

incidentally, Stanley Wolfe had attended as a youth). He drove a Ford Econoline. (He later told federal agents that he had thought all along there was something "funny" about the activities of the Wolfe brothers, and his somewhat furtive trips to Oceanside, but had never thought to ask any piercing questions; this young man, one feels, perhaps symbolizes the attitude of many Americans toward the illicit but profitable activities of nonviolent professional crime. Besides he was paid between twenty and fifty dollars per trip—"off the books.")

Two or three times weekly the young college student drove the green Econoline to a poorly lit parking lot in Oceanside. The lot was located at the end of Hampton Road on the south shore of Long Island, and when he got there he met a "Joe" or a "John." From one or the other he received the goods, which were loaded onto the van, and a shipping order made out to Cedarbrook Fashions of Philadelphia. In the unlikely event that the Econoline was stopped by police, the young man was protected with superficially legitimate cover. The student signed the shipping orders himself.

Each trip, the student brought back to Philadelphia between 19 and 36 individual cartons, each carton worth an average of $400 wholesale. This meant that each trip was worth wholesale an average of $8,000.

Back at Cheltenham Avenue—the trip took about three hours; the college student was cautious and never went over the speed limit—the truck was unloaded, sometimes under the direct supervision of Stanley or Nathan. The shipment largely contained varieties of women's and children's clothing, with various other items thrown in, such as handbags, shoes, and even some men's clothing.

The first order of priority, after the goods were removed from the truck, was to destroy the shipping labels on the boxes. These indicated the true owners of the merchandise. Usually these labels were placed in the trash at the rear of the store.

About every other week Nathan Wolfe boarded an Amtrak train from the 30th Street station in Philadelphia for New York. The purpose was to meet Stracuzza, discuss future shipments, and pay for previous ones. Often Nathan met with Mario Stracuzza right in the middle of the lobby of Penn Station, and often paid in cash in a brown envelope.

Stracuzza was thus the bagman as well as the middleman. He split the money four ways. Nick Simone, the floorwalker, received one share; the two trucking firms another share *each;* and Stracuzza himself up to a share, though sometimes less.

Between October 1972 and February 1973, each of these four individuals appeared to clear thirty thousand dollars in cash. This estimate is based on the assumption that the Wolfes paid 40 percent of wholesale price for the sequestered merchandise. Federal agents assume that roughly three hundred thousand dollars' worth of Volume Merchandise clothing was channeled to the Wolfes during this period. Assuming that the Wolfes fenced the stuff at 90 percent of wholesale to their receivers, it is possible to conjecture that the Wolfes may have cleared roughly $150,000 over the same period.

There was always some disagreement among the parties as to the exact value of the merchandise, however. For many items none of the parties knew precisely what the stuff was worth. While Stracuzza, Simone and the trucking executives speculated among themselves, the Wolfes had a much more scientific method of determining price.

One thing they did was to look in a wholesale catalogue. For them, as for many other fences around the country, the Sears Roebuck wholesale catalogue was their Bible.

For other items, the Wolfes simply picked up the phone. They figured: Who would know better the wholesale price than the manufacturer himself.

Occasionally this procedure required a ruse.

To illustrate, on February 23, 1973, Nathan Wolfe needed some prices. The merchandise at hand was the manufacture of the Dun Knitware Company. After obtaining the firm's phone number from Information, Nathan, ensconced in the tight second-floor office on Cheltenham Avenue, picked up the phone.

"Hello, I'd like to have the salesman for the Boy's Division," he said.

"This is he," said the voice on the other end in New York. "Who is this calling?"

"This is Alper's in Atlantic City, New Jersey."

"Alper's?"

"Right."

"Okay, go ahead."

"There's a couple of style numbers I'd like to know about, if you still have them, and how much they are."

"Okay, go ahead."

"Uh, nine oh seven."

"What?"

Nathan is straining to read the numbers off the stolen garment box. "Uh, what is this down here—nine one oh? She has written down here, it looks like nine oh seven, nine one oh."

"In boys'?" The salesman in New York is assuming that "Mr. Alper" is having trouble reading his secretary's writing.

"Yeah. Do the boys' come in extra large?"

"Yeah, but are you talking about the imports?"

"That's right."

"Nine oh seven is a vinyl import."

"Acrylic."

"Acrylic, right, but it's with vinyl trim."

"That's it."

"That's a pullover with a half zipper."

"That's the one."

"Yeah, we have some, but you didn't buy any, did you?"

"No," said Nathan, "I didn't buy, but my girl was up there and wrote down these numbers."

"Oh!"

"I'd like to know if you still have them and how much they are."

"Nine oh seven," said the salesman, "is forty-eight dollars."

"Less eight . . ."

"No, that's net."

"Forty-eight net?"

"Right."

"All right, now, nine one oh."

"Nine one oh is forty-eight dollars."

This is really all Nathan needs to know. However, he finishes up with a charade to avoid suspicion.

"All right," he said. "I'm going to be up there Monday, uh what's your name, sir?"

"At what hour?"

"About eleven . . . That's too early?"

"No, that's fine."

"Uh, what's your name, sir?"

The salesman gives his name.

"Okay, Mr.————. I'll be there Monday."

"Okay, your name is Mr. Alper."

"Right, Alper. A-L-P-E-R."

"*Alper.*"

"Right."

"Okay, thank you."

"Thank *you.*"

Armed with the wholesale price, the Wolfes then calculated their own selling price to their retail outlets. The price varied between 50 and 90 percent of list wholesale. In no case, of course, did their price equal wholesale. The whole point of dealing with the fence is that he can get it for you for less than wholesale.

The Wolfes' receivers were scattered throughout the United States. By picking up the telephone they were in touch with old customers in such far-flung places as Secaucus, New Jersey; Chelmsford, Massachusetts; Brownsville, Texas; San Diego, California; and Birmingham, Alabama. The phone was their greatest ally; between February and May of 1972, for example, they made from Cedarbrook Fashions office more than 334 calls to 42 cities in 17 states.

Whether or not their receivers knew what was going on is highly debatable. They may just have assumed the Wolfes were shrewd wholesalers. They may have known exactly what the score was. Either way, they probably didn't care. "Got any more of those good buys?" was the frequent line receivers used when checking in with Nathan and Stanley. One reason for their lack of concern is that the Wolfes' receivers always received a receipt for their purchases. "They know that no court in the land," explained one federal agent, "will prosecute a businessman if he got a receipt. They know it, we know it."

Persuading a receiver to take merchandise off their hands at less than wholesale was the easiest part of the entire operation, as this long distance call to Texas on February 21, 1973 suggests:

"This is Cedarbrook Fashions in Philadelphia," said Stanley.

"Right, how are you? What's cooking?" answered the Texas businessman.

"Well, I've got a new shipment in of acrylic pullovers here, with vinyl trim and half zippers. Very good stuff. You interested? They're Dun of New York."

"Well, how much?"

"For you, forty-three per unit."

"Hold on a minute."

Here the Texan was probably consulting his wholesale catalogues.

"For two dozen, forty-three dollars?" This price is 10 percent below wholesale.

"That's it. The price is right?"

"The price is right. I'll take four." He means four units. The two parties discuss future possibilities.

"I'll keep you informed if anything comes in."

"Thanks."

Stanley usually made the sensitive phone calls, letting Nathan deal with flunkies like Stracuzza.

Once, however, Stanley dealt with Stracuzza personally. Concerned about the quality of the merchandise he was getting from Nick Simone, he decided to try to apply a little heat.

The conversation took place on February 22, 1973.

"Listen," said Stanley, "try to talk to him [the floor manager].

Tell him to keep [i.e., put aside] the women's wear . . . because there's more money in it."

Stracuzza mutters something in his defense.

"Look, I want to explain it to you."

"Go ahead."

"The other shit"—he's referring to ladies' handbags and belts and so forth—"there's no money in it, even if you get a whole truckload of stuff."

"Well, I tried to speak to him."

"You got to try to get at least ten- or twelve-dollar stuff." Wholesale price.

"This other shit, it not only makes no money, but it's harder to get rid of—you know what I mean? Like for instance, they [Volume Merchandise] got, like, raincoats coming through, they got coats, you know, this is where the money is."

"Okay."

"There must be a way. I don't know how this is done but there must be a way where you get the right stuff. . . ."

"I got to put the pressure on them, because they know what goes in the box [that is, the truck to Oceanside]."

"Right, this is what I am saying. . . . It's ridiculous, it's ridiculous to throw away all that effort. You get half as much for the same goddam effort. . . . With the same effort you can take a box that got ten times the value."

"Okay, right."

Stanley also dealt with potential suppliers. Although he had a good thing going with the Volume Merchandise deal, he constantly sent out feelers for new sources of merchandise. In this conversation, Stanley was talking to a relative of his who had an influential position in New York's garment district. The subject is summer dresses, and Stanley is at the phone in the back office of Cedarbrook Fashions on February 22, 1973.

"Let me ask you something," said Stanley. "I need a lot of summer dresses, you know, with names on it." (Identifiable brand tags.)

"With what?"

"With names, you know."

"Oh, yeah."

"Maybe you can get me some summer. I just want summer, you know. . . . Quite a few, quarter-sleeve and sleeveless."

"Three quarter, you mean?"

"Yeah, and pastel color only, you know, either polyester or Arnel . . . Know what I mean? Pastels only?"

"Yeah."

"This is what I'm most interested in, mostly misses' and women's. I'll take juniors' but I really need misses'. Maybe you can make some sort of deal, you know, with somebody you can work something out with. That's all, *I don't have to know where you're getting it from.* (Italics mine)

"Okay."

"Label merchandise is what I'd like to get. However, if they want to take out the labels I might go along with them. Do you know what I mean? If we get a good enough price."

"Yeah, I know what you're talking about. How many do you need?"

"I can use five thousand dresses," Stanley said.

"When do you need them?"

"I have until the end of March to get them."

"To the end of March?"

"Right, I got to let this guy know who's called me whether I can deliver."

"Yeah."

"In other words, he wants to know if I can get him five thousand dollars' dresses, you know what I mean. Then he can come here in March."

"Right."

"Maybe you can set up a deal with a guy. Know what I mean? A cash deal."

"All right, I'll check into it. . . . I think we can."

At this point Nathan gets into the conversation on the office extension.

"You know what it is, *Nichols* wants five thousand dollars' dresses at twelve dollars each."

"Nichols!" The New York party sounded surprised at the mention of a well-known chain store.

"Well," says Nathan, "he is willing to pay twelve dollars."

There is a short pause on the line.

"What about," says the party, "what about slacks and pants?"

"No," replies Stanley, "I'm not interested in. . ."

"No, no," yells the party from New York, "I mean, can *you* get *me* pants?" In this ironic switch, the New York supplier is proposing to the fence that he supply his New York firm with merchandise. The supplier wants to become a receiver, at least on this one deal, and the fence, of course, swings both ways. Stanley says he'll look into it.

1. *Without the fence, there would be no thief.*

Basically, the thief needs the fence to survive. The thief's fund-raising abilities would be greatly diminished were the multiconnected fence not around to handle the fruits of his crime. Indeed, the very existence of the fence is considerable encouragement to the thief, who then knows where his next meal is coming from. What's more, some fences actually act as controllers, putting out orders to one thief, telling others to cool it, giving out instructions to yet others about how to bring home the merchandise.

2. *Without the thief, there would be no fence.*

Most fences do not appear to be your basic stick-up men. They leave the real dirty work to others. If others weren't up to it, the work might not get done, and there would be no goods to fence. Of course, the fence does sometimes help to set up crimes.

3. *Without the receiver, there would be no fence.*

The fence requires the willing consent of the retail businessman to survive. If the businessman weren't always on the lookout for the criminally cheap product, the fence would have to close up shop. Whether the receiver is in fact guilty of crime is not as consequential as the fact that no receiver ever asks of his supplier the kind of hard, searching questions that necessarily should be asked. So there is clearly a conspiracy between the good guys and the bad guys, and in this context at least not a qualitative difference between them.

4. *Without the receiver, there would be no thief.*

Your average thief does not have enough contacts in the legitimate world to handle all he steals. But he needs the buyer. He can only use so many color televisions and women's overcoats himself. And the buyer, for understandable reasons, wants to insulate himself from the dangerous thief, especially if he is a legitimate person running, for all appearances, a nice, clean business. Thus the fence is the agent for both the thief and the straight.

5. *The fence and the receiver actually run the show.*

They are paying for the crime.

The master fence is the most elegant underworld creation of all. He may receive a stake from organized-crime figures to use his connections in the legitimate world to move stolen property for them, and will arrange the deal so that he will never actually come into possession of the merchandise. The master fence is the hidden arranger for the crime world, and he is well rewarded for his connections. In testimony before the Senate Select Committee on Small Business, this exchange took place:

> CHAIRMAN: "Now are there master fences in New York City? Chief fences, big fences, whatever you want to call them?"
>
> THIEF-WITNESS: ". . . Well, off hand, I know four big fences that can come up with a hundred thousand in cash, no sweat."
>
> CHAIRMAN: "Four big fences that can come up with a hundred thousand in cash?"
>
> THIEF-WITNESS: "Yes."

The one-hundred-thousand-dollar figure somewhat understates the volume of business. As a rule of thumb, a fence would have to handle at least three quarters of a million dollars in stolen merchandise to earn one hundred in profit. Thus, four master fences in New York City alone are handling perhaps four million dollars a year in stolen merchandise.

No one knows how many fences there are in the country, and no one can even make a decent guess. However, one's imagination is stimulated by the knowledge that fences deal in an astonishing array of merchandise—everything from credit cards, securities, stolen or forged documents (car registrations, licenses, passports, to mention just a few), steel office equipment, airline tickets, clothing, shoes, meat, appliances. The fence is the American connection.

CHAPTER FIVE

Crime Pays

THIS MAY WELL prove a troubling chapter to many Americans. For it will indicate how much money can be made by a professionally dishonest person. Unfortunately, as you will see, crime really does pay.

At the outset, it bears stating that underworld salaries not only are comparable with those in other industries, but, because of the tax dodge, actually are superior in many categories. It should not be surprising, then, that the crime profession regularly manages to attract to its ranks some outstanding talent. This infusion of fresh young blood helps the underworld maintain its edge in its war on legitimate people.

The Internal Revenue Service, for example, has estimated that the underworld annually accepts about twenty billion dollars in wagers—admittedly, a conservative estimate—and that about 6 or 7 percent of this gross is retained as pure profit. This handsome profit margin helps to underwrite the high salaries and enticing commissions of the underworld employee.

Most criminals work on commission. Thus, ultimately, the criminal's income depends on how hard he works and the take on each job. Sometimes the number of jobs over time fluctuates wildly, making annual estimates difficult.

Here are some brief sketches showing how much money some successful professional criminals can make in the various rackets.

NUMBERS RUNNER

A numbers runner is in the employ of a gambling combine. His work role is to accept bets from people in their homes or places of employment. His income is based on a percentage of the take. The actual take depends somewhat on the organization he's working for, but in general he gets between 15 and 25 percent of all bets he takes; from 33 to 50 percent of the losses of a new customer; and a 10 percent tip from the customer when he or she wins. If a numbers runner handles five hundred dollars in action each day, then his daily salary, as it were, would be roughly one hundred dollars. (This is an absolutely tax-free sum.)

BURGLAR

The burglar also works for a percentage of each score, the difference going to the fence, or criminal receiver. Burglary income varies tremendously. One Dorchester, Massachusetts, burglar manages only fifteen thousand a year, plus welfare; a New York burglar, who lives in Westchester County, and who commutes to New York once or twice a week to commit his foul deed, does considerably better. Here is how he did during 1972. The information is based on an interview conducted by a friend:

In January, four scores for a net (after overhead, largely the occasional tool or transportation cost; most of the merchandise was fenced) of two thousand; February, three scores for thirty-five hundred; March, five scores for twelve hundred; April, three scores for two thousand; May, three scores for three thousand; June, three scores for one thousand (a bad month); July; two scores for four thousand; August, none (vacation); September, one score for three thousand; October, two scores for two thousand; November, one score for six thousand; December, none (vacation).

Total income for 1972 for this Westchester County burglar was $28,700.

Again, this is a tax-free sum. Twenty-eight thousand dollars of untaxed income is the spending-power equivalent of perhaps forty thousand dollars, at today's tax rates. Forty thousand dollars is a tremendous salary in this country. I know of bank vice-presidents who make considerably less than that.

To cover up illicit income, many criminals bank a large percentage of their profit and live more or less on welfare or unemployment. So the average American is hit in two ways: he not only is deprived of tax revenue from the criminal, but in some cases has his tax money appropriated for the purpose of paying the criminal's welfare checks.

JEWELRY FENCE

This is a highly specialized occupation. There are not too many of them, and most of them are simultaneously legitimate businessmen, that is, they run their fencing operation out of a regular jewelry store or exchange. Also, in New York and several other big cities, the jewelry fences exist at the sufferance of the reigning syndicate executives; in this way, any big jewelry heist in that city has to be approved by the bosses, who naturally take their cut (more of this later), because if it weren't, the burglars would have great difficulty fencing the take.

Jewelry fencing is highly profitable. One big fence on the West Side of Manhattan reportedly cleared three hundred thousand one year—just on fencing.

PORNOGRAPHY STORE CLERK

This one is a real shocker. In New York, along 42nd Street, there are dozens of dirty book and peep-show stores. Many, if not all of them, are owned by organized crime interests. A simple clerk in these stores can earn up to five hundred a week in straight salary, plus a percentage of the gross after a certain level. He is also provided with a lawyer in the event of a bust. So, if he works for a full year, as many do, then splits for Europe or the West Coast, he makes twenty-five thousand a year—the equivalent of perhaps a taxable income of thirty-eight thousand for a single man, under current schedules.

MUSCLEMAN

A muscleman is usually a member of the enforcement area of a criminal outfit. His job is to enforce law and order, as the bosses so define it. Some musclemen work on a free-lance basis—that is, they are known as leg busters and hit men, and so on.

How much a muscleman actually makes depends, obviously, on how active he is. For breaking a man's leg, a muscleman will charge anywhere from one hundred to a thousand dollars. For serving as an armed guard on a robbery team—i.e., riding shotgun —a man can get one hundred fifty dollars for an hour's work. For protecting an organized crime card game for a night, one hundred dollars. For a straight hit (murder), the cost varies from a thousand dollars to fifteen thousand. The very best hit men value their services exorbitantly, so that the fifteen-thousand figure is probably closer to the average. However, a contract killer who is on the payroll of a criminal organization may not get anything per hit— just his salary, which will probably be in high five to low six figures, easily.

LOAN SHARK

"Loan sharking," Angelo De Carlo, the New Jersey mobster, once said inadvertently into an FBI tape recorder, "is the strongest racket in the world . . . better than numbers or anything else, and cleaner."

By "better," the convicted gangster meant "more profitable:" A good loan shark puts one hundred thousand dollars out on the street in loans to hard-up addicts, businessmen, criminals, and so forth, and by the end of the year realizes a pure profit of one hundred and fifty thousand dollars.

This is because of the interest rates. The usual loan-shark interest on a loan is 20 percent per week. If I borrow one hundred dollars from a loan shark, I pay him twenty dollars per week until I pay back the original principal. (See chapter 8.)

On a longer-term loan, I might pay 1½ percent interest per week, or 78 percent a year.

Established loan sharks are easily six-figure-a-year professionals.

STREET PEDDLER OF DOPE

Once again, tremendous variation here. Often this man or woman is just scraping by.

MARIJUANA IMPORTER/WHOLESALER/RETAILER

One marijuana entrepreneur I know also holds down a full-time job as a drug salesman with a pharmaceutical firm. In this capacity, the young man is a traveling salesman. He sells over the counter for his firm and under the counter for himself. He clears about thirty thousand dollars a year, and much of the money is stashed in out-of-state banks.

We should note, morosely, that salaries in the straight world are generally not so good. Besides, anyone who is on salary is subjected to the cruel straitjacket, the income tax system. The only people who seem to be able to beat this system, then, are the very rich, or the crooks. Of course, in some cases the two are identical.

CRIMINAL SALARIES
(Estimates based on the experience of successful criminals)

Job	City	Estimated Annual Gross
Peep-Show Clerk	New York	$20,000 (tax-free)
Hotel Burglar		
(Pick Man)	East Coast	$75,000 (tax-free)
Pickpocket	Miami	$20,000 (tax-free)
Numbers Runner	Harlem	$26,500 (tax-free)
Numbers Controller	Brooklyn	$60,000 (tax-free)
House Burglar	Long Island	$25,000 (tax-free)
Burglar (Industrial)	Westchester County	$75,000 (tax-free)
Bank Robber	East Coast	$24,000 (tax-free)
Shoplifter		
(Booster)	Washington	$15,000 (tax-free)
Drug Distributor	Los Angeles	$27,000 (tax-free)
Hit Man		
(contract, non-		
salaried)	Chicago	$75,000 (tax-free)
Loan Shark	New York	$125,000 (tax-free)
Drug Importer	Miami	$165,000 (tax-free)
Pornography		
Store Owner		
(sex shows, films,		
magazines)	New York	$120,000 (tax-free)
Mob Lieutenant	New York	$125,000 (tax-free)
Securities Thief		
(airports)	East Coast	$100,000 (tax-free)

These figures are rough estimates of the gross income of fourteen successful criminals for a minimum of one year over the last five years. They are not mean figures, averages, or necessarily even representative incomes. In fact, they were chosen precisely for the purpose of illustrating the point that crime can indeed pay. The estimates, in each case, used at least two sources, and usually three, to arrive at the income over a one year period. Usually one of these sources was the criminal himself. In all instances, the estimates are skewed toward the conservative figure, and the final list was circulated among professional criminals and law enforcement officials in an effort to make sure that none of the data is out of line. Of course, the list must be read with some skepticism. It is impossible to determine beyond any possibility of doubt the income of a criminal, if only because by necessity his income gathering remains secretive. I.R.S. statements, even if they were available, would be unrevealing. Still, as gross estimates for working criminals, the list is as factual as it can possibly be made and, at least among the experts to whom it has been shown, well within not only possibility but more importantly past experience, as revealed by I.R.S. cases against professional criminals. Also, several of the figures in the chart were coordinated with published testimony, including Congressional hearings on organized crime. For instance, in the hearings before the Permanent Senate Subcommittee on Investigations in June of 1971, a criminal convicted for mail theft gave testimony regarding his activities as a securities thief. (His testimony was corroborated by a staff member.) "My share of the loot my partners and I stole in a four-year period," he said, "came to approximately $1 million." This would average out to $250,000 per year. However, professional criminals consulted argued that this (1) seemed too high and (2) was not in the least representative. On this basis, the experience of another criminal, who admitted to an average income of $100,000, seemed more appropriate for the chart. In the same vein, I have quoted one professional drug distributor in Los Angeles as making $27,000 a year. Virtually all sources, on both sides of the fence, suggest that this figure might be misleading, since it seems relatively low. However, it is a real figure, and I rely on the general thrust of chapter 6 to remind the reader that a great deal more money is regularly made in drugs.

. . . AND NOW FOR THE OVERHEAD

Criminals are the first to argue that their overhead costs are just like those of any other business. These costs are somewhat more bizarre than those, say, of the corner delicatessen. But the principle is the same—which, in plain English, is that you can't get something for nothing.

A list of these costs that a criminal might bear in mind include monetary ones as well as those that cannot possibly be measured in dollars and cents.

PSYCHOLOGICAL OVERHEAD COSTS

Davey* is so paranoid that he hates to walk to his car. He gets up in the morning and thinks, Maybe I can do everything by phone, never have to leave the house. Then he remembers that his phone is tapped—or so he thinks. Maybe, he thinks further, I shouldn't

---

* Davey is not his real name.

even get out of bed. Then he remembers that this is no use either: the police have planted a bug in one of his bedposts—or so he thinks.

Davey is a typical narcotics criminal. There are thousands of them in the trade, and just about all of them, understandably enough, have the same complaint. I'm being bugged, I'm being watched, I'm being followed, I'm in big trouble. What can I do? They look at a utility repairman on a telephone pole and see an FBI man taking notes. They see a suspicious guy at one end of the bar and won't even go to the men's room, because it'll give the man a better shot at him.

This is the paranoid world of the professional criminal. Now, there are overhead costs and there are overhead costs. It may be that the ones that cannot be quantified into dollars and cents are the most painful of all.

Sometimes crime exacts a tremendous toll. The fear of detection and arrest can be a living hell. Perhaps the price is worth paying, perhaps not. But it is one that professional criminals pay all the time.

Of course, Davey doesn't do what seems obvious, I think, to you —that is, get out of the business. The money is just too good to be true. Last year he managed to clear one hundred thousand dollars, after expenses and other overhead costs. Still, there's no way of measuring the psychological toll on Davey over the long run.

The psychological wear and tear come from not knowing what lurks around the corner. The straight businessman who goes to work every day, puts in his eight hours five days a week, comes home bored, perhaps, but at least he has the satisfaction of some security against sudden, absolutely unexpected turns in fortune.

The criminal has no such psychological security. He is at the mercy not only of his luck on the job, but also of the police, and of fellow criminals as well. If a professional criminal trespasses on another criminal's territory, there may be consequences. Criminals suspected of informing police face instant retribution if discovered. Criminals who are truly doing well in their line of work face the jealousies of those who are not. Although the crime business is not as violent as portrayed in television and movies, still, it is entirely possible that some frustrations may be vented at the end of a gun barrel.

The question of whether there is honor among thieves is important in this context. Among criminals who respect each other greatly there is a considerable sense of mutual integrity. But among relative strangers and outright competitors, there is very little of the Ten Commandments indeed. This is why Davey says, "Whoever said there was honor among thieves didn't know what he was talking about." Davey feels this way perhaps because in the drug world there are so many newcomers to the business that there is no sense of community whatsoever. In more established trades, the situation may not be quite so bad.

Here again, there is an exception to the rule. For some reason, the bookmaking business seems rife with animosity and subterfuge. As an investigator of organized gambling in the State of New York once observed, "Bookmakers cheat not only the public but one another. As one bookmaker stated, he would never trust the word of another bookmaker. Bookmaking partnerships are notoriously fragile, with constant changes in personnel. Some bookmakers absolutely refuse to deal with certain others. Bookmakers give one another false odds and point spreads. . . . They inform police against competitors not approved by organized crime whom they wish to drive out of business." With minor modification, this general description of the bookmaking business applies to the drug world as well.

For all this, criminals seem prepared to pay the psychological overhead costs in return for what they regard as relative freedom from the straitjacket of the normal world. The very thought of a nine-to-five job reassures the criminal that he is doing the best for himself after all. And, remember, the vast majority of these criminals making very good money indeed have no higher education whatsoever. In fact, many of them have no lower education to speak of, either, and would be limited to low-paying menial jobs were it not for their involvement in crime.

I recall once being on a talk show in New York with the brilliant crime novelist George Higgins, himself a former assistant United States Attorney in Massachusetts and an exceedingly knowledgeable person about the criminal life. The hosts of the show were two very nice ladies who, I believe, were adept at throwing teas among New York's higher society. At one point in the discussion, one of the hosts complained that she could not understand for the life of her why any young man would become a criminal. George Higgins then asked her what she would do if *she* had a choice between an $80-a-week job as a car-washer or a three-hundred-dollar-a-week job as a numbers runner. The fine lady said she'd definitely be a car-washer. Then she asked Higgins, who is as quick as he is direct, what he would do.

Said Higgins, "I wouldn't work in the car wash."

THE OFFICE HOURS OF THE CRIMINAL

Day Burglar (apartments, homes)	11 A.M.–2 P.M.
Night Burglar (hotel)	6:30–11 P.M. (dinner and theater hours)
Night Burglar (house)	12 A.M.–5 A.M.
Booster (department store shoplifter)	12 P.M.–2 P.M. (crowded lunch hour)
Fence (general merchandise)	Any time (but especially 5 A.M.–12 P.M., when the hijackers come in)
Drug Dealer	Any time (but especially on weekends, when federal narcotics cops are off)
Mugger	11 A.M.–2 P.M. (old ladies shopping) 5 P.M.–7 P.M. (tired secretaries) 12 A.M.–4 A.M. (inebriated businessmen)
Auto Thief	Anytime

THE POLICE

Here we break down the overhead cost into several categories.

First, there is the complete police investigation. This can cost the criminal a great deal, especially in lost time; the criminal getting wind of the trouble ahead may simply leave town for a long vacation. This can be tremendously costly to the criminal whose business has built up a certain momentum. (Usually, the criminal will go right about his business, hoping for the best.) Then, there is the police bribe. This can be measured in dollars and cents and, indeed, is often an integral part of an operation.

In the past few years police investigations have gotten quite sophisticated. The police have been forced to upgrade themselves, in part by court decisions restricting gang-buster techniques that served in the past, in part by the growing sophistication of the professional criminal. In any event, full-scale police investigations now are almost entirely restricted, in the big cities, to major criminals.

Criminals in narcotics, burglary and even gambling can still do a modest business and not draw the boys decked out in the utility-man overalls on a telephone pole across the street, tapping the phone, or the technicians in the panel truck with the peephole shooting Vista-Vision films. But as the size of the business increases, the criminal has to realize that he becomes a plum for the cops.

Here is what can happen to a criminal, assuming the cops in his area are *not* on the take.

1. The police can open a preliminary investigation. This will entail a record check, some interviewing, a few phone calls to registered informants (of which all municipal police forces have thousands)—that sort of thing.

2. Police initiate visual surveillance. This means they are serious. Police don't generally sit in unmarked cars for hours upon hours unless they are onto something. This is usually the beginning of the end.

3. Police obtain authorization from a judge to wiretap or bug a suspect's office or home. In order for the police to be permitted to use wiretap testimony in court against the defendant, the police must first obtain a court order for the electronic surveillance. Of course, nothing can stop the cops from putting in eavesdropping equipment without a court order if they want to; and if the purpose

is simply to find out what the criminal is up to, they can always go to the judge for official approval of a second tap. However, putting in a tap or bug without a court order is strictly illegal, but some cops do it all the time. Whether the electronic surveillance is authorized or not, however, the use of this equipment means that the investigation is deadly serious and that the cops won't give up until they've got something—if only to prove to their bosses that they knew what they were doing and to justify the expense of the surveillance, which is very high.

4. Police will work on an associate of the criminal. They will make an incriminating case against this associate, then offer him a deal. In return for testimony against the guy he is working for—the higher-up—the police will see to it that the prosecutor and the judge are lenient.

For the police, this is a terrific deal. They nail a lot of criminals this way. They get the smaller fish to point the accusing finger at the big fish, like John Dean, the former White House counsel, making accusations against President Nixon.

There is only one problem with this kind of deal. Sometimes the smaller fish invents his story. To get himself off the hook, he weaves out of whole cloth an incriminating tale about another criminal, on whom police have placed a high priority. Sometimes police and prosecutors even coach the accuser, helping him to invent his damning story. Of course this is unethical but it is done a great deal. Ambitious prosecutors often descend to the same level as the very criminals they seek to incarcerate. For example, in the thirties, Lucky Luciano, the boss of the American Cosa Nostra, was set up in this way. He was indicted and convicted on the charge of fostering white slavery, or prostitution. The prosecutor was Thomas E. Dewey, later to become Governor and even later Presidential nominee of the Republican party. Luciano was guilty of many violations of law, but one thing that was beneath him—as it remains beneath top-level criminal bosses today—is the prostitution rackets. A former high official of the New York Police Department once admitted to me that Luciano had, in fact, been "set up."

5. Police sometimes go one step further. They actually plant incriminating evidence on the premises of the criminal. This is common in narcotics cases. They break into the criminal's residence or place of business, plant a stash of dope, return the next day with a search warrant, discover (surprise!) the damning evidence, and arrest the suspect. They will do this because

a. they know that the criminal has been doing such-and-such, but they have not been able to catch him red-handed and are frustrated.

b. they are shakedown artists; they will use the planted evidence to elicit a bribe.

c. they are absolutely desperate for an arrest because the pressure is on from headquarters for a "crackdown" or the captain has been breathing down their necks for the past few months or they are genuine law-and-order nuts who believe that any means justifies the end of putting the bad guys where they belong, behind bars.

6. Police do nothing even slightly unethical and go to the district attorney with absolutely hard, professionally obtained evidence. In this event—and it is an event that does occur—the criminal had better get himself a good lawyer. When the cops actually take the trouble to put together a good, clean, thorough case, they can do one tremendous job.

Taps and bugs are the criminal's true bane. When a piece of listening equipment has been legitimately installed, it can be devastating. Although many criminals today insist that they no longer converse freely on the phone, or even in the office, some of them must, because the cops keep putting taps in, and they keep picking up some great stuff on the tape recorder.

Here are a few excerpts from a wiretap transcript. The tap was put in under court order. The New York detective had gone to a judge, with the district attorney at his side, with a so-called wiretapping affidavit. This is a long, tortuous document, which seeks to justify to the judge violation of the citizen-suspect's Constitutional right to privacy. The affidavit contains a summary of the investigation, the alleged activities of the suspect, and the reason why electronic surveillance must be used. In the particular affidavit from which these quotes are taken, the detective adds portions of a transcript from a previous tap. I found these excerpts fascinating, and I pass them along to show you not only how criminals talk to one another, but how detailed is the information given a judge on an application of this sort.

Excerpt One

The detective, in the affidavit, explains to the judge that in recent months there has been a relative shortage of heroin on the street in New York. Then he quotes from a conversation between two Cosa Nostra narcotics dealers about the shortage.

> FIRST DEALER: "I don't know, we doing something wrong, or what? I don't know what the fuck it is."
>
> SECOND DEALER: "I don't hear of any—I don't hear of anybody scoring. This Jack says, 'Forget about it, it's clean,' he's clean out. Anybody scoring, maybe one. They bring it around in person."
>
> The detective explains to the court that "I don't hear of anybody scoring" means that the Cosa Nostra member doesn't know of anyone obtaining large amounts of narcotics, and that the only people actually receiving narcotics are getting it from criminals who operate independently: "Anybody scoring maybe one [that is, one kilogram], they bring it around in person."

Excerpt Two

The detective also pointed out to the judge that this was a sophisticated trafficking organization, and that the members sought to insulate themselves from lower-level dealers who might be under police surveillance. In this conversation, we see that the dealers are not very happy about having to associate with a certain Jack, who it turns out is a heavy narcotics user and who has several times been arrested.

> DEALER THREE: "We gotta worry about Jack. I told him to call only in an emergency, you know."

DEALER TWO: "Yeah, 'cause he got in trouble and every-thing."

DEALER THREE: "So I made him drive me downtown. Then I say, 'You dirty cocksucker, I told you [inaudible] only in an emergency. The only fucking thing you worried about is whether I got something or not."

The detective points out to the judge that Jack apparently had called up to inquire whether he could buy some dope.

The dealer's irritation with "Jack" was further expressed in an overheard conversation on September 29, 1972, around nine o'clock in the evening.

NUMBER TWO: "Jack wants five. I was going to give him the whole five tomorrow, okay?"

NUMBER ONE: "I wouldn't."

NUMBER TWO: "Well, I say let's do it. He's got headaches. They're on him all the time. He's got the I.R.S."

UNIDENTIFIED MALE: "I.R.S.?"

NUMBER TWO: "Yeah, he's on the spot."

NUMBER THREE: "I.R.S."

NUMBER TWO: "It's [the heat is] all on this guy, all on this guy."

NUMBER ONE: "You know, I hate to see, I hate to see it happen, so many times [inaudible] . . . fall out a fucking window, I swear to God."

NUMBER TWO: "He should run away, didn't we tell him that?"

Incidentally, they never did execute Jack. The cops arrested him before they had the chance.

The simplest way of dealing with the cops is to buy them off. Many criminals believe that most cops can be persuaded from duty by a percentage of the take. In return for the bribe, the cop either sabotages an ongoing investigation, fails to complete an arrest, makes an improper arrest—deliberately, so that the case will be thrown out of court—or offers testimony at the trial in such a way as to undermine the credibility of the prosecution's case. I say this is the easiest way. Given the cost of today's lawyers, it may also be the cheapest.

Criminals often take out insurance policies, or licenses, with the local precinct. In return for a percentage of the action, the criminal enterprise is insured against arrest or is guaranteed adequate warning in case of a headquarters-ordered crackdown. The insurance policy is called a "pad" by the police, and in some police forces the pad is regularly collected, a representative of the police actually making the rounds of the clientele much like a newsboy collecting for his papers.

The chart of the next page is an historic document. I have seen very few like it in my research. Yet I am sure it represents absolutely typical criminal bookkeeping. Ordinarily, a profit-and-loss statement of a gambling combine, complete with entries for "payoffs to police," would get burned before the police raided. This one didn't. In figuring the picture today, allow for the enormous decline in the value of the dollar over a thirty-year period.

THE GAMBLING BUSINESS IN HISTORICAL PERSPECTIVE: THE OVERHEAD COSTS
The Balance Sheet for Gambling Operations in Cook County, Chicago, for the month of July 1941.

(Until uncovered by investigators, this sheet was seen only by Jake Guzik, Frank Nitti, Edward Vogel and Murray Humphreys, four top underworld leaders)

1. Gross earnings from slots, gambling houses, et cetera in Cook County outside of Chicago

$322,966

2. Overhead cost/Payoffs to Police, prosecutors, politicians

$ 26,280

3. Net profit (gross minus all overhead, including payrolls and graft)

$221,674

4. Annual Projections:

Gross	$3,875,592
Projection	315,000
Projected Net	$2,660,000

NOTE: The records consisted of six sheets of loose-leaf ledger. The bribe takers were noted in code, such as "Skid," "O.G.," "Tub."
SOURCE: *Chicago Tribune,* October 25, 1941.

Some criminals pay off the police in information about other criminals, rather than in money. These informants, who are well situated in the profession, meet regularly with police officers, usually detectives, to brief them on news of the underworld. In return, the cops may issue these informants what is in effect a license to operate. These licenses are issued only to *productive* informants. As a result of this information, it may be said that a very high percentage of police arrests of professional criminals can be attributed to information from these licensed criminals.*

Thus a certain percentage of the criminal world in a metropolitan area is not only known to the police, but subsidized by them. This percentage is in effect an arm of the police department. A certain percentage of every burglary, every narcotics transaction, every hijacking and so forth is not only known, but tacitly approved, by police officers.

ATTORNEY'S FEES

Upon arrest, the criminal immediately secures an attorney. If the criminal is unconnected with a formal crime organization, then he'll have to retain one himself. Otherwise, the ring will provide one. A major fringe benefit of being attached to a ring is the automatic appearance of the ring's attorney at your arraignment. Even criminals who are not so affiliated tend to have a lawyer on retainers so they don't have to fish around at the last minute.

The attorney's fee probably constitutes the most expensive overhead cost of the criminal life. Very good criminal lawyers are *very* expensive. One attorney who represented an East Coast fence in 1974 was rumored to *start* his fee in a major criminal case at $25,000. One professional criminal once told me that in his opinion, the real criminals in the American way of crime are the

---

* The number of criminals actually licensed by police to make a living in this way is quite extraordinary. This is primarily because in the United States there is so much activity in the crime world that the police can barely keep up with it all. Without the help of these double agents, the police would be totally left behind.

criminal lawyers. "They never lose," he said. "The more crime there is, and the more court cases, the more money they make. The guys really making the dough in this game are the lawyers. My son asks me what he should be when he grows up, I tell him go to law school and be a lawyer so I can retire early on his first million."

It can even be claimed that the high cost of legal talent contributes to the frequency of crime in America. On the face of it, it is an astounding, even incredible argument, but it is one that criminals make frequently. It goes something like this (I am paraphrasing an acquaintance of mine from Miami who deals in dope):

"You get busted, the first thing to do is to find a good shyster lawyer. He's going to cost a lot of bread. Where do you get the bread to afford a high-priced lawyer? You go out and score. I sell dope, another guy steals a car, another guy a bank. Add it all up, and you got these fancy lawyers making for a new crime wave. And don't think they don't know it. Why do you think they keep asking for postponements and adjournments and all of that legal crap? To give their client more time to get up the bread, that's all. They're going to make a deal with the D.A. anyway, rather than go to trial. All they care about is their fee. And they know there's only one way for us to get it, and that's do our thing. And don't tell me to go to Legal Aid. Those guys are for the birds. I know one Legal Aid lawyer, he told his client where to find a fence for his next job. . . . Listen, everyone is in this thing together. Lawyers, crooks like me, judges, it's all one big game."

Precisely what lawyers do with their exorbitant fees puzzles some criminals. The cynical ones—that is, most criminals—believe that where the fee is $25,000, the judge gets about ten thousand and the prosecutor five. How much truth there is to their allegations has never been proven. Although one hears in courthouse circles rumors that such-and-such a judge can be "reached," evidence supporting the allegations is almost always nonexistent.

Whether or not some judges are corrupt, the fact is that criminals do tend to go to jail from time to time, their sentence being the major nonmonetary cost of doing business. Usually their lawyers seek to negotiate a light sentence for their client in return for pleading guilty. Usually such requests are granted. Criminals' trials are generally quite lengthy, and exceedingly costly, and everyone involved in the criminal justice system seems to prefer the easy way out by reaching an out-of-court settlement. In a sense, the plea-bargaining system is a game of mutual bribery. The criminal bribes the prosecutor and the judge by offering to save them a lot of trouble; the judge and prosecutor bribe the criminal by offering to save him some time.

Plea bargaining is an atrocious perversion of justice and should be halted immediately. Even criminals secretly agree with me that plea bargaining is a joke.

JUDGES AND THE COURTS

Criminals are not deterred by stiff sentencing or harsh laws. When a stiffer narcotics law was put into effect in New York State on September 1, 1973, proponents of the tough law predicted that in short order the drug dealer would be forced out of the state. On the face of it, the prediction seemed reasonable.* The penalties for dealing were the harshest in the nation, and it was thought that by raising the drug dealer's cost of doing business, he could be driven out of business. In actuality, the theory behind the law was reasonable, but the calculation was naïve; what happened was that in comparison to the profit in the drug trade, the overhead costs were being only marginally increased. Crime still paid in New York for

* On the contrary, I would argue that longer prison terms are undesirable precisely because prison contributes to crime rather than cures it. Prisons are not rehabilitation centers, but graduate schools in crime. They do not make the bad guy into a good guy, but reinforce every criminal instinct and talent that the offender has. If a man enters prison as a relative amateur, by the time he comes out there's a very good chance that he has been converted into a professional by peer-group pressure, as well as the opportunity to learn new tricks of the trade from the accomplished performers.

the narcotics dealer, even if the overhead went up somewhat. Indeed, there is some reason to believe that the higher overhead costs were simply passed on to the drug consumer in the form of higher retail prices for heroin, cocaine and marijuana.

If the possibility of prison shapes the behavior of criminals in any respect at all, it is perhaps in their choice of line of work. Criminals are very much aware of disparity in sentencing and will take several factors into calculation, if possible, before embarking on a score. One factor is the likelihood of detection and conviction for the crime in the area in which they are working. Another is the estimated sentence they will receive upon conviction.

In New York City, for example, there is a tremendous difference in both these factors, and criminals try to keep up on developments. They do this not by reading *The New York Times* or scholarly studies of sentencing, but by reflecting upon the experience of unfortunate colleagues.

One sentencing study in New York shows the possibility of a jail term per type of crime and the likely sentence for that crime. One such study showed that between May 1 and October 31, 1972, if you had been convicted in federal court, you would have had the following chance of going to jail:

If Caught and Convicted and the Crime Was	*Chances of Some Sort of Time Were*
Securities Theft	100%
Bank Robbery	83%
Narcotics Trafficking	77%
Bail Jumping	67%
Rackets and Extortion	56%
Interstate Theft (hijacking, etc.)	55%
Counterfeiting	52%
Guns, Sale of	50%
Gambling	37%
Income Tax Evasion	35%

In the following chart, which professional criminals are generally aware of, the list of offenses is arranged in a different order. This list tells the criminal what the average sentence was per violation.

If the Crime Was	The Time Was (Average)
Bank Robbery	70 mos.
Narcotics	62 mos.
Securities Theft	57 mos.
Rackets and Extortion	47 mos.
Guns, Sale of	28 mos.
Interstate Theft	18 mos.
Counterfeiting	15 mos.
Bail Jumping	10 mos.
Income Tax Evasion	6 mos.
Gambling	3 mos.

Please keep in mind that these charts refer to the experience of criminals who are *caught*. Most professional criminals are *not* caught.*

The balance sheet shows the following:

1. Many crimes pay well.

2. The payoff is enhanced by the fact that the take is off-the-books; the money is tax-free. Every dollar in criminal take is the functional equivalent, for argument's sake, of at least a dollar fifty in legitimate income. (I recall once going out on a raid of a "massage parlor" with police. As one officer was handcuffing one of the girls, he said to her, "Why don't you give this all up and come work as my secretary at the precinct house?" The girl, who could not have been older than twenty-one, laughed and replied,

* The figures presented above are statistical means and averages. In reality, there is a tremendous disparity in sentencing in the federal courts, and professional criminals know this better than anyone. A recent study of fifty federal judges in New York, Connecticut and Vermont illustrated the dimensions of the problem. A questionnaire was distributed to the judges, who were requested to sentence a number of hypothetical cases. In one "case," a union official was convicted on a nine-count extortion indictment. Under law, he could have received up to twenty years on the main charge, and up to $75,000 in fines. One judge "sentenced" him to the full twenty years and $65,000 in fines. Another levied a mere three-year sentence and no fine at all. Judges who are routinely "soft" on certain crimes are deliberately sought out by criminal lawyers—that is, every effort is made to get their client's case before the least punitive jurist for the particular offense in question.

"Sure, if you'll pay me five hundred a week—and *off the books!* —sure.")

3. The overhead costs are sometimes exceedingly high, especially in terms of personal freedom, but the money is good, too. When the criminal balances the equation, he comes up with the result that profits exceed overhead (and venture capital) costs by a margin sufficient to make the profession very attractive indeed.

4. Unless the overhead costs can be made staggering beyond belief—and it is difficult to see how this might be done consistent with the Bill of Rights—profits will always exceed overhead. Crime will pay.

CHAPTER SIX

Short Cuts

NOT LONG ago the illegal drug scene was very different from what
it is today. During my college days the key underworld figure on
campus was my pusher friend Jimmy.* He sauntered around campus
typically hungover from a combination six-pack high and marijuana
headache, looking, by the way, not at all unlovable in his standard
uniform of Athletic Department sweatshirt, tattered sweatpants,
and red sweatsocks. This young man wasn't, of course, a professional criminal; he was a campus character.

The difference today is the difference between a Mom-and-Pop
store and a nationwide retail chain. The illegal drug trade is a 75-
billion-dollar-a-year international business. In major cities and
suburbs across the United States, it is the source of employment
for literally tens of thousands of criminals. If Jimmy were "in the
life" today—he's retired—he'd probably have several thousand
dollars in the bank, some real-estate investments, and a working
knowledge of dope-dealer Spanish (for frequent runs into Mexico
and South America). Quite a few people have made their fortunes
in America's dope business.

Contrary to the belief of some experts, the Mafia does not have
a monopoly on the trade. It is basically a wide-open business, with

* "Jimmy" is not his real name.

a complex of interests and groups that are alternately competing against and complementing each other. In one instance a South American exporter may sell to a Cuban middleman located in Miami for delivery to a Mafioso in New York—an inter-ethnic delivery. In another case, narcotics from the Far East under the supervision of Sicilian criminals will be routed through Canada to the United States in a race against a similar Asian package routed through Lima under the care of Peruvian suppliers—*both* for sale in the lucrative New York-Chicago dope market. Occasionally, tempers flare, guns go off, and a dope war ignites, but, by and large, the market is so enormous that there is more than enough business to go around.

Actually, there is not one dope market, but at least three. There is, first, the heroin-methadone market; the consumers are mostly addicts and are drawn largely from the lower-middle class. To support their habit, crime becomes their second habit, usually the petty, street-level variety.

Secondly, there is the soft-core drug market; the consumers in this category are not addicts, by and large, but otherwise well-integrated Americans with money to spare; largely from the middle and upper-middle classes, their tastes range from marijuana to cocaine (a nonaddicting stimulant of the leaf of Latin America's coca bush), and occasionally amphetamines and methamphetamines (varieties of speed, a synthetic stimulant).

And then there is the so-called pill market; the consumers here are quite often superficially well-integrated middle-class and usually suburban Americans; their indulgence turns to pills of all descriptions for all sorts of real and imagined needs, especially depression and sleeping problems.

The dope entrepreneurs differ strikingly as well. The average heroin tycoon is a veteran criminal affiliated, if not actually pledged, to a stable smuggling ring or formal crime organization.* As for

* At latest count, there were twenty-six Mafia crime families in the United States, and at least an equal number of non-Mafia crime families involved in everything from illegal drugs to loan-sharking and gambling. The organi-

coke and marijuana (the two drugs are linked not by any pharma-cological kinship, but by the preference of the users), here there is no *average* type. The dealer, supplier and importer may well be an entrenched professional criminal, or he may be a free-lancer with a university Ph.D. from a good, respectable American family (the doctorate is often in chemistry, perhaps not surprisingly). Fre-quently he is a participant in the so-called rock counterculture, and his associates are not known criminals but musicians, actors, song-writers, actresses and poets. And in the pill-for-every-ill category, the pusher is very likely to be a licensed physician, dispensing drugs under the counter at highly inflated prices.

Though there is considerable overlap of these categories, a com-plete blend has not yet taken place. And, pending a total change in the nation's drug laws, differential association among the three types of entrepreneurs and markets seems likely in the foreseeable future.

Some pushers I talk to, however, sourly predict that ten years from now distribution of many of these drugs will be taken over by legitimate corporations chartered by the government under radically revised drug laws. It is believed that even morphine and heroin (the latter a chemical refinement of the former) will be available on the open market. It is an unpleasant thought for criminals, of course, because legalization will not only take the outrageous profit out of the trade, it will take all of the profit out of the trade *for them*.

There is simply no way for the average free-lance entrepreneur to compete against a big American pharmaceutical company in the open market.

Until the millennium, the black market drug trade will remain the most extraordinarily profitable business in the world of crime, and marijuana will remain the number-one drug of choice.

---

zational basis of most of these outfits is ethnicity, resulting in Chinese-American gambling rings, black dope rings, Cuban smuggling organizations, and, of course, the usual, all-purpose Italian-American crime family with interests in a variety of rackets and countries.

Marijuana (a/k/a *grass*) is the leading seller among all illegal drugs. According to estimates arrived at by the Senate Internal Security subcommittee, thirty-five million Americans have used marijuana at some time, and more than ten million are regular users. This 1974 estimate means that marijuana regulars account for fully 5 percent of the population of the United States of America. This is a tremendous commercial market.

The situation is ideal for the professional criminal. Legitimate businesses are deterred from supplying the commodity because of its illegality; the criminal businessman, obviously, is not. What's more, the actual social hostility to use of marijuana is so weak that it gives the drug entrepreneur the best of both worlds. On the one hand, the drug can be marketed at artificially high prices because of the black market conditions attributable to the drug's illegality. On the other, the tacit consent of the very people whom the law against marijuana was designed to protect simplifies the marketing problem and reduces overhead insofar as the police are involved (in that community support for harsh action against heroin dealers, say, does not extend to marijuana, which is perceived as a much lesser evil). Of course, if marijuana were not illegal, it would be sold competitively on the open market.

Marijuana is today an international business, and it is considerably more organized than is generally suspected. Although the profit margins are not as high as in the harder drugs, like cocaine and heroin, the volume of sales is so great that the industry is more or less on a mass production footing. And one tip-off that the trade is an organized activity comes from the fact that prices tend to be uniform throughout the United States. As one drug trafficker told me, "If you try to undercut the market, you won't last long."

This suggests that organized crime enforcers are involved in the once innocent pot business. A rash of recent killings in the South, especially Texas, probably stems from the elimination of competitive and nonprofessional elements in the trafficking. During 1973 and 1974 Italian organized crime figures began appearing on the marijuana-trafficking scene, which as I have suggested was the exclusive province, once upon a time, of amateurs, romantics and small investors.

Although Moroccan and other varieties of grass are available in the States, the big exporters of marijuana are Jamaica, Mexico and Colombia. The shipment of small amounts of marijuana from these locales to the States can be handled by just about anyone, but the shipment of large amounts requires considerable wherewithal and mechanical paraphernalia. In Jamaica, the marijuana is farmed in fields up in the high mountains far from the island nation's few urban centers. (This is also where the famous Jamaican high-mountain coffee is produced, not to mention the exquisite Royal Jamaican cigar tobacco.) These marijuana fields are huge but fairly well camouflaged, and there are so many of them that it is entirely possible that the number-one cash crop of Jamaica is not bauxite, as the official travel brochures suggest, but *ganja,* as marijuana is called in Jamaica.

Ganja-growing is a major source of income for Jamaica's criminal class and for a few members of the Parliament. It is not surprising, under these circumstances, that the police have been relatively ineffective in stamping out *ganja* production, an ineffectiveness enhanced by the fact that a considerable percentage of the Jamaican police force smoke marijuana themselves on a regular basis.

The transport of Jamaican *ganja* to the States is conducted primarily by small plane. I once stood at the edge of a Jamaican *ganja* field as farmers were preparing to ship some one hundred pounds. I had been in Jamaica on a magazine assignment and had gotten in touch with *ganja* traffickers through the well-known ruse of looking like a naïve tourist and hanging around in places where my relatively well-tailored clothes and American face would most likely attract attention.

For this particular story, the place to hang out at was a bar at the Norman Manley International Airport outside Kingston, the capital of Jamaica. After a few rounds of planter's punch, I let it be known to the bartender that I was looking for a local "guide" to show me around town that night. A wide, all-around naïve smile and a small bill for the bartender were all that were necessary to prompt the attention of one sharp young man at the bar.

After some preliminary conversation, the guide ascertained my true interest, which was visiting a *ganja* farm in the Jamaican countryside, and for a surprisingly modest fee, was more than happy to serve as my host.

(How did he know I was not a law-enforcement agent? There are some tricks in the profession of journalism that must necessarily remain more or less out of the public domain, but the fact is that any good investigative reporter would have had no difficulty in seeing for himself the most famous *ganja* fields of the Caribbean.)

The next afternoon, I picked up my guide in my rented Toyota with left-hand drive. The drive to the *ganja* farm took almost four hours, and along the way we passed what must rank as some of the most beautiful scenery in the world. By the time we reached the farm, it was nightfall, and exceedingly hard to see. It was then that I began to wonder if I had made a mistake trusting this young man next to me, a complete stranger and a self-admitted hustler since the tender age of eleven.

It turns out that there was absolutely nothing to worry about. When we got to the farm, we were met by two guards with carbines on their shoulders, but the guns were meant not for me but for unauthorized intruders. In fact, the guards and then later the farmers seemed glad to see an American journalist, who, they felt sure, was likely to give their product some good publicity back in the States —their primary market.

We were taken to a small farmhouse where the owners lived, offered some rum and Jamaican grass (which, like Jamaican cigars, is strong and pure-tasting), and considerable conversation. Then, close to daybreak, we were ushered out to the edge of a small, makeshift airstrip. The strip was nothing more than a thin swath of clearing cut into the hillside. Two laborers had packed the grass into two canvas bags, and set them down on the edge of the strip. We waited.

At about daybreak, a two-engine Beechcraft 2400 came down out of the skies and roared onto the clearing. The plane slowed down to a halt but never did stop. In virtually one motion, the native farmers ran up to the plane, a side door opened, and two sacks of grass were shoved on board. The plane moved on, gathered speed, and roared up into the sky. The destination was a small landing strip in the south of Louisiana, where grass distributors from the States were anxiously awaiting delivery of the precious cargo. The plane flew low as it crossed the Mexico–United States border to avoid radar.

This is not a bush-league operation. In fact, at one time in Jamaica there was so much small plane traffic because of the *ganja* business that traffickers actually installed a radio tower on top of a mountain in order to help guide the planes in for safe landings, especially at night. (The tower was finally removed by police.) It is exceedingly probable that some of the importers in the States were connected with organized crime outfits; for one thing, the traffic was so heavy and continuous that a great deal of front money was involved, and this sort of money is not available to most individual entrepreneurs; and, for another, I was told by Jamaican traffickers that Mafia elements in the States were paying Jamaican criminals for the grass not in dollars, in some instances, but in small arms, especially handguns.

The title of this chapter is Short Cuts. This is because drug trafficking provides ambitious young criminals with an express route to great fortune. There has been nothing like it since the Eighteenth Amendment (Prohibition), which was responsible for the development of a criminal class in the United States on an absolutely unprecedented scale. It is manifest that today's drug laws are having the same profound effect on the size and shape of our contemporary criminal profession as the laws against alcohol had in relation to the burgeoning of organized crime. It seems to me that in the twenties Prohibition brought into the profession of crime a great number of minority groups, especially Italian, Irish and Jewish elements. Today, it further seems to me, the drug bootleggers are also largely minority elements—to wit, black, Latin (especially Cuban), and white-university. These constitute the fresh blood in the criminal profession.

Let me illustrate, with two very unusual white-university-type criminals.

Cynthia is the kind of blonde who seems always to have a tan. She is about twenty-two, almost six feet tall, and vivacious. I was introduced to her by a business associate of a friend of a friend of mine; this associate is a Cuban émigré who operates on the periphery of cocaine and marijuana traffic in the United States. Cocaine is a psychotropic drug that is one step up from marijuana in the sense that marijuana users seem to gravitate to coke far more readily than to heroin, a much harder and viciously addicting drug.

Cynthia is part Cherokee, I think.* At least this is what the associate told me. He knows many operators in the drug trade. Cynthia, he said, was a dealer.

She is also a dancer, topless, in a commercial establishment in a major East Coast city. The place is quite a dive, actually (the men's room has probably never seen soap and water). Its chief attraction, obviously, is the presence of Cynthia, which is luminescent. She is a fairly recent dropout from a well-known city university.

When Cynthia is not dancing at the club, her boyfriend takes her to the Caribbean, where she likes to play at the tables of the gambling casinos. As for professional activities, she was getting rich—but not from dancing.

"I get thirty dollars a shift, plus tips. So I make fifty a day, usually."

"That's not too bad."

"Then I make five hundred a week on dope."

* Her real name is not Cynthia.

"How's that?"

"I sell, maybe, forty pops a week."

"Coke?"

"Right."

"Forty tins a week, that's twenty-five dollars a tin."

"Right."

"How much do you pay for the stuff?"

"Five hundred."

"And you clear five."

"Yeah, except some of it I use myself."

"So sometimes less than five, maybe some weeks only two or three hundred, plus the dancing, which is a bonus."

"Yeah."

"So, really, the club is just a good place for scoring. If you couldn't score, maybe you wouldn't dance."

"Right."

"Do you use coke while you work?"

"Yeah, and speed, too."

"Really?"

"Ever look at a dancer and notice her eyes?"

"Yes."

"Hard and sexy, right?"

"Yeah."

"Wrong. She can't even see you, especially if her contacts are out. She's doped up. That's why her eyes are so hard. She gets doped up so she can dance for eight hours straight and can forget where she is. But the guys think she's getting turned on to them, but really it's the dope."

With that, Cynthia got up for her twenty minute set. It was her turn to dance. When she took her top—a black cape—off this time, I noticed there were no needle marks on her arms. So no heroin was being used. I also noticed that she was looking at me with sexy, hard eyes. Had I not known better, I would have assumed it was pure love.

Then there is the case of the twenty-seven-year-old employee of the City of New York, a bright Jewish boy for whom his job as a welfare inspector was not sufficient to support him in the style to which he wished to become accustomed.

In 1973 the District Attorney in Bronx County, New York, announced the arrest and indictment of sixty-one young people in connection with the operation of an international cocaine-smuggling ring. The ring smuggled into the United States each year some six hundred pounds of cocaine, four thousand pounds of hashish, and various other drugs whenever and wherever available. The ring purchased the coke in various Latin American centers, such as Bogotá, Colombia, and then arranged for air transportation of the merchandise to Mexico City. From there, the coke was sequestered across the Mexican border, into Texas or California, in the clothing and private parts of female couriers, usually young American college girls out to make some bread. Once in the States, the couriers were met by agents of the ring, who distributed the precious organic stimulant in various places around the country.

What shocked newspaper readers was the disclosure that the head of this multimillion-dollar ring was a twenty-seven-year-old welfare inspector named Howard Zachary Fuchs. To quote the announcement of the indictment, "Mr. Fuchs was born and raised in Bronx County and educated at Yeshiva schools. He graduated from Yeshiva University in 1968, and from then until June 1972, he was employed by the New York City Department of Social Services as an investigator."

This tremendously successful dope dealer lived in a luxury apartment on Manhattan's chic East Side, owned a suburban residence in Scarsdale, New York, and drove around in a $14,000 Citroen-Maserati. At the same time, Mr. Fuchs, according to the announcement, had set up a number of seemingly legitimate corporations with the coke profits. He also was alleged to be the secret owner of a number of campus bars around the country, where presumably his coke could be sold under the counter even as the beer and whiskey flowed over it.

One of Fuchs's East Coast principal lieutenants, according to the district attorney, in announcing the indictment, "was Michael Arlen, twenty-nine years of age . . . Mr. Arlen is a part-time actor, having had minor parts in various daytime soap operas including 'Secret Storm,' and has also appeared in some commercials for television."

The indictment indicated that Mr. Fuchs had made numerous trips to Bogotá to set up deals and described the many methods of smuggling the coke out of South America. In one instance two of his aides were taxied in at a private airport on San Andres Island in the Caribbean. As they prepared to take off with twenty-two pounds of coke aboard, they were arrested by American and Colombian officials.

At the conclusion of the indictment, District Attorney Mario Merola noted caustically, "The average age of the members of the cocaine ring was twenty-five. The oldest was thirty-one, the youngest twenty. . . ."

This pattern is a national one. In addition to the entry of black, Chinese and Latin traffickers into the drug business, which is a major new development in professional crime in the United States, we see the rise of white-university elements. They begin in the marijuana and pill trade, then graduate into cocaine and other hard drugs. I think it will only be a matter of time before we see their money reinvested into areas such as loan-sharking (criminal usury) and the organization of prostitution. (Already, white-university prostitution is a growing business in some cities in the States; this suggests that the girls come to you with a university degree or perhaps dropout status.)

The entry of young people into the criminal world via the side door of drug traffic is exceedingly unsettling to the older, more-established members. On the whole, the involvement is tolerated, though hardly encouraged, and it is my belief that young entrepreneurs like Fuchs will find it difficult to survive on a grand scale in the underworld, because of the opposition of organized-crime elements. It is one thing for a young man to score a few kilograms of coke or a ton or so of grass. But as the quantities increase, so do the profits, and the established money-makers do not welcome other success stories. It is my belief, though I cannot prove it, that Howard Zachary Fuchs's arrest was prompted by underworld information supplied to the authorities. In essence, this is a form of hit-man action; instead of the crime syndicate (in this case, New York Mafia) calling in an outside gunman to get rid of Fuchs, a salient piece of information is supplied to the police, and the effect is the same as a hit—the entrepreneur is taken out of action. This is a very common practice in the underworld; criminals who are not, for whatever reason, welcome in the criminal fraternity are routinely given up to the police.

The old-timers vigorously support this sort of counterattack on the white-university counterculture involvement in professional crime. I became acutely aware of the intensity of this feeling one evening in a bar in downtown Chicago. I was sitting at the bar nursing a Martini (my own drug of choice). Next to me was Jack,* a professional criminal who has done just about everything— loiding, picking, hijacking, fencing. Everything except drugs. He doesn't like the stuff, doesn't want to get involved in the business, but is extremely annoyed at anyone who is making a fortune overnight in the trade.

Jack expressed his feelings about young men who take this short cut to a fellow professional standing at the bar with him. Both these men were dressed in sports jackets and sports shirts, and were looking pretty dapper. This place was a singles bar (the two criminals were hoping to score a couple of young Chicago secretaries).

The conversation, condensed and as best I recall, went like this:

"First," Jack says, "the kid gets bagged on a GLA [Grand Larceny Auto—a typical involvement for an up-and-coming criminal]. But he wasn't too cool about it. He steals the same car again."

---

* "Jack" is a pseudonym.

His partner roars with laughter.

"So the cops pinch him, he goes to the judge, the judge slaps his wrist."

"Suspended sentence?" asks the friend.

"Right. Now the cops aren't too happy about this, right? So they do a number on him, beat the shit out of him."

"Taking justice into their own hands. Tsk, tsk. Didn't these guys ever hear about Miranda and Escobedo?"

Jack laughs. "Well, anyway, this makes the kid as sore as hell, so he goes to a distant uncle. Guy named Tony Scabs."*

"Well, well," says the friend, admiringly.

Then Jack explains that Tony Scabs tells the kid to see a Cuban on the other side of town.

"Tony Scabs sends him to a Cube named Skinny Rodriguez, who's in coke. Skinny sends him to Detroit. Next thing you know, he's on American Airlines to the Caribbean."

"To score some coke?" says the friend.

"Right. Three keys.† Hard to believe, isn't it. Well, the kid wanted to get back at the cops for beating him, so he brings back three fuckin' keys."

"So he makes a bundle."

"Figure the Cube gives him one to two grand a key, seeing as how the kid's from Tony Scabs."

"Nice score," says the friend.

"Don't forget the suntan."

"It's not right, you know, it's not right."

Jack sipped his drink and reflected on the number of times he scored five or six thousand dollars that easily. He didn't tell me,

---

* This is not the actual name used. And if there is a Tony Scabs in Chicago, it is pure coincidence. This is a made-up name to protect me from trouble on my next trip to Chicago. "Skinny Rodriguez" is also a pseudonym.

† A key is short for a kilogram, or one thousand grams, or, roughly 2.2 pounds. One key of coke can be purchased for a few thousand dollars in Latin America and retailed for twenty to twenty-five thousand dollars in the United States.

but I had the distinct impression that the number was not very great. Stories of young criminals coming into the underworld and scoring large sums of money overnight are a tremendous source of resentment among older criminals.

There is now a generation gap in the criminal world. The traditional career paths to profitable positions in the profession are being scrapped by youngsters with get-rich-quick schemes. The primary short cut is through illegal drugs. As long as the dope industry is a relatively wide-open game, their path will become a well-traveled route to the pot of gold at the end of the rainbow. Perhaps it already has. However, the older, more-established criminals know where the trafficking routes are located; should they decide to put up roadblocks, the primary concern of young dope entrepreneurs won't be the cops. It will be the older, harder bad guys.

The law then is really the drug businessman's best friend. Without it, he would be as absolete as a bathtub still. Because of it, he has it made.

The profit structure of the heroin distribution industry on the East Coast illustrates what is at stake. Here is an industry in which profit-making is so extraordinary that the criminal must go to sleep at night praying for the continuation of anti-narcotic laws.

Let's look at the upper levels of this industry for the purpose of seeing exactly whom the law helps.

At the upper levels, there are three major occupations. There is the importer. There is the wholesaler. There is the major supplier.

The importer is the Mr. Big. Sometimes he is so big that the little fish at the bottom of the industry don't even know his name. In New York, prior to 1972, he was very likely a high-echelon member of a Mafia family, arranging for delivery of as much as a hundred kilograms of narcotics at a time (this is an exceedingly large amount of narcotics). After 1972, the industry was severely shaken by the arrest of key figures, and the disruption of the primary heroin route (Far East to Marseilles to New York). For a while much smaller shipments were the rule. However, by 1975, with Turkey resuming full-scale production of opium, and with the rise of Latin smuggling rings with a capability to transport European heroin as well as home-grown cocaine, large-scale transactions were once again possible.

The importer is the big man, because he deals in such large gobs of money. In 1970, for example, a top lieutenant in the Mafia family of Carmine Tramunti acted as the family's primary heroin importer. He was a middle-aged veteran of the criminal world who knew all the ropes. In the early part of that year this lieutenant dispatched an aide to Europe to confer with established exporters. The European exporters owned a refining laboratory (which converts raw opium to finished heroin) in the north of Italy, and imported opium from Turkey twice a year.

For this deal, the Europeans offered the Americans a delivered package of forty-five kilograms of pure heroin (Turkish) at $7,000 a kilo. At a crowded restaurant in downtown Milan, the criminals shook hands in agreement.

The Mafia importer in New York now had the problem of raising $315,000 in payment. But for a top lieutenant in a Mafia family, it was no problem at all. A man in his position has several alternatives; among them are (1) using his own resources and (2) soliciting backing from other members of the family, who may themselves be heroin wholesalers, so that their initial contributions will be regarded as deposits against final delivery.

In this case, the lieutenant reached into his own pocket. It may seem incredible to most of us, but this is well within the means of upper-level members of organized crime. Once, when another member of the Tramunti crime family was informed by a police officer that $400,000 worth of hijacked goods had been recovered by police, the *capo* (lieutenant) said, "$400,000? Big deal. I make that every week." Of course, the criminal may just have been bragging.

When the heroin reached the port of New York, the importer

contacted five New York-area wholesalers. These were organized crime figures with whom he had successfully dealt before.

The importer offered the wholesalers the heroin at $15,000 per key, in a nine-key package. The package came to $135,000. None of the five wholesalers had the slightest difficulty meeting the price. As a result, the importer grossed $675,000. For his efforts, which may have taken a month or two at most, the importer makes a profit of ($135,000 times 5, minus $315,000):

$360,000.

Now the wholesalers went to work. As a rule, the wholesaler tries to sell his stuff as soon as possible (like the fence, he is uncomfortable in the possession of hot goods). He usually sells only to established customers (if you or I went to him and tried to buy a few keys, we might be lucky to emerge from his office in one piece) and usually will not dilute the heroin with adulterants. Adulteration occurs at a lower level, the point of the process being to puff up the quantity and thus the profits. (Incidentally, during Prohibition in the twenties, a similar cutting process took place: the liquor was watered down to spread it around.)

These general rules were followed to the letter in this deal.

None of the wholesalers had trouble unloading his heroin. One wholesaler, for example, sold four keys to a Jewish supplier and five to a lower-level Mafioso. In each instance, the price per key was $24,000. This means the wholesaler, on an investment of $135,000, grossed $216,000. Thus, for a few days' work, involving coded telephone messages to the key principals, the wholesaler makes a profit of ($24,000 times 9 minus $135,000):

$81,000.

Next, the major suppliers. These may or may not be formal members of a crime family. They may be drug independents, or simply big-time free-lancers.

In the 1970 case, the major supplier who purchased four keys from the wholesaler moved to cut his product. To cut is to dilute. To dilute is to deal in quantity rather than quality. So far, the importer and major suppliers have been dealing in 90 percent pure heroin. The major supplier is about to change all that. To the four keys of pure heroin the supplier added eight keys of quinine and milk sugar. This produced twelve keys of watered-down heroin (roughly 30 percent pure). The cost of the adulterants was roughly a thousand dollars.

Then, the supplier repackages the newborn twelve keys into forty-eight quarter-kilo bags of 30-percent heroin. Next, he sold each of these bags at $7,500 a piece. (Of course, the drug is cut at least once before it reaches the streets.) Thus, for an initial outlay of $96,000 for the four keys to the wholesaler (plus $1,000 for the adulterants), the gross income is $360,000. For his efforts, the major supplier on the deal clears in profit—

$263,000.

Can there be any wonder that the narcotics laws have attracted criminals?

There has been a change in the method by which trafficking organizations smuggle narcotics. This change is a reflection of improved police activity against narcotics smugglers. The traffickers have been forced to modify their methods in the wake of large busts, such as the French Connection case.

THE OLD WAY

The story I want to pass on to you began on a street corner in southwest Miami, in the Little Havana section of town, in the summer of 1970. It was on that street corner that Rudolfo Quintanilla and Jorge Vazquez met, entirely by design. Rudolfo Quintanilla was a professional criminal and, in the argot of the smuggling trade, a *stash man,* who lived and worked the narcotics business in Miami. Jorge Vazquez was from Santiago, Chile, and represented some Latin American traffickers. He was the organization's paid enforcer.

A stash man and an enforcer are key principals in any large-scale smuggling operation. The stash man provides a hiding place for the narcotics as it is en route from its source to its intended purchaser. The enforcer acts on behalf of the supplier and rides shotgun, as it were, on the shipment. He makes sure that when the narcotic is delivered to the buyer, the buyer delivers the money.

Rudolfo Quintanilla evidently had involved himself as a stash man in previous shipments of narcotics to Miami, a central trafficking center in the Western Hemisphere and perhaps the most important port of entry to traffickers in the United States. About twenty-five, he wore modish clothes, wore his hair chin length, and kept a small cottage at 44 Santillane Avenue in southwest Miami, as well as an apartment on the other side of town. The apartment was for living and entertaining; the cottage was for harboring narcotics from Latin America en route to New York. Jorge Vazquez was in his middle forties and had been arrested in 1967 by Frence Sûreté on charges of theft, illegal use of passport, and the passing of bad checks. He was a five-foot-five-inch-tall bruiser with a tattoo on one of his forearms. If Rudolfo Quintanilla could pass as a lead guitarist in a rock band, Jorge Vazquez was Central Casting's choice for the role of the hardened smuggler.

Part of Rudolfo Quintanilla's responsibilities was to introduce Jorge Vazquez, as the organization's representative in Miami, to the other partners in the smuggling. These introductions took place mainly at the Dupont Plaza Hotel in downtown Miami. Here Vazquez met his back-up as enforcer, a Chilean named Carlos Rojas, and the money courier, Marcos Osorio. The money courier is the man who will return to the supplier with the payment. Osorio was a forty-five-year-old man and, according to the information provided by federal sources, a veteran of the São Paulo rackets.

In this case, the supplying organization was located in Santiago, the capital of Chile, where the exporting of cocaine is among the city's most productive activities. And the receiving organization was a New York Mafia family. Between the supplier and the receiver, however, stood a Cuban organization headquartered in Miami, where Cuban émigrés, many with C.I.A. training from the

Bay of Pigs days, conduct high-level narcotics transactions. In recent years Cuban traffickers have become central elements in the international narcotics business. They finance, transport, receive, distribute and organize drug traffic.

In this case, the Cuban middleman was Andreas R. Rodriguez, a well-placed individual in the Cuban criminal community. It was believed by federal narcotics agents that this Cuban trafficker had previously conducted major drug deals with leading New York criminals. Rodriguez allegedly had in the past been involved in three separate coke shipments totaling thirty kilos. (At his level, coke was running perhaps eight thousand per key.)

In personal appearance, Señor Rodriguez was a stunning departure from the usual Cuban criminal style. Rodriguez was a flashy, stylish dresser who kept a separate apartment for entertaining and partying. Most Cuban criminals dress well, but not conspicuously. Unlike their counterparts in black crime, the Cuban is exceedingly nonflamboyant in almost everything he does. He is not a Superfly impresario, and the car he drives is likely to be a five-year-old four-door sedan chosen deliberately for its inability to attract the eye. To look at him or his wares, one would not think that his annual income from crime is a six-figure sum. He does not flaunt it. One has to be impressed with the Cuban criminal style, which undoubtedly helps to account for the success of many Cubans in professional crime, especially smuggling.

At one meeting at the Dupont Plaza Hotel, Rodriguez revealed to his co-conspirators that one of the buyers was actually in a hotel room in Miami waiting for the stuff. The buyer was Blackie Calabro, identified by law-enforcement authorities as a New York Mafioso.

On the night of July 17, 1970, a meeting took place which was ultimately to decide the fate of the smuggling operation. At the bar of a superb Cuban restaurant on Southwest Fourteenth Street in Miami known as the Bilbao, four people discussed business over drinks.

The first person was Ada Villanueva. About forty, she was a loud dresser, a Cuban woman reportedly with contacts in the coke and heroin traffic along the Latin American to Miami to New York run. The second was her business associate Andreas Rodriguez. The third was a six-foot, 170-pound good-looking American; and the fourth his companion, a skinny, blond, five-foot-seven-inch Italian-American male.

The two men had patronized this bar on several occasions in the past. Each time they were in the company of "good people," that is, Cuban-Americans with underworld connections. The "good people" had always introduced them to the bartender, and to anyone else who would listen or was interested, as "good people from New York"—meaning Mafiosi.

Actually, the two men, who evidenced interest in buying large quantities of cocaine, were federal narcotics undercover agents.

On the night of July 24 in a hotel room at the Dupont Plaza, Rudolfo Quintanilla, the Miami stash man, held his first organizational meeting.

It is believed that Jorge Vazquez and Marcos Osorio were at the meeting. It is further believed that the group agreed to rent a white late-model Ford for the switch car, that the car would be left at a specific parking lot near Miami International Airport, that the keys to the car would be left under the front seat, and that the car would be left at this certain place at ten in the morning for a period of no more than four hours.

Osorio, the money courier, took down the details and somehow relayed them back to the trafficking organization in Santiago.

On July 26, Andreas Rodriguez drove to the Patricia Hotel in Miami and called on a man in room 710.

It is believed that the man who answered was Blackie Calabro, the New York Mafia wholesaler, and that in the envelope he passed to Andreas Rodriguez was a cash payment in six figures. This was the front money, representing 50 percent of the total purchase price.

On the night of the twenty-sixth of July a million-dollar cargo finally came down from the sky. In the hold of a lumbering C-46A

Curtiss-Wright cargo plane were two hundred pounds of cocaine as pure as the driven snow.

The plane was the flagship of a small but active Chilean charter cargo line. It had landed at the commercial aviation facilities of Miami International Airport around midnight after leaving the Dominican Republic, its last previous scheduled stop. Its pilot was a man named Oscar Squella-Avendano, the president of the airline and, according to the judgment of a federal jury a few years later, the ringleader of the trafficking organization.

The next day, July 27, the small-airline executive and his mechanic and co-pilot woke up in separate motel rooms at the Arrowhead Motel in downtown Miami, got in their rented car, and drove to Aerotrade Incorporated, a spare-parts warehouse about one half mile from the airport where their plane was hangared.

After picking up a part and putting it in the trunk of his rented car, the ringleader walked around the block to the corner of Tropic and Fairway drives. At that corner was a small, ten-car parking lot where the Chilean had presumably been instructed by his money-courier by phone the night before to pick up the white Ford.

The ringleader got into the car, drove back to the warehouse, picked up his mechanic, and headed for the C-46 with the million-dollar cargo in the hold.

When they got to their plane, they first decided to do some repair work on one of the engines, after which they taxied the plane to the end of the runway to rev up the defective engine. After a half hour of this, during which the federal narcotics agents with binoculars were hiding in the grass outside the airport fence positively dying of suspense, the two Chilean traffickers taxied back to the hangar.

Then they unloaded the dope. The coke was packed in cardboard cartons in the hold of the aging plane. To get it, the executive had to hoist himself into the hold, and hand down the boxes one by one to his trusty mechanic, who then placed them into the rear of the white Ford he backed up to the plane. In a matter of some fifteen minutes, roughly a half dozen boxes of cocaine, total two hundred pounds, were secured in the trunk of the car.

Then minutes later the white Ford was back in its spot.

Then the two Chileans walked back to the parts warehouse and left in their own car.

At two-twenty that afternoon a '68 Dodge circled the block near the parking lot several times, as though wary of being observed. Driving the car was Rudolfo Quintanilla, the Miami stash man, and in the passenger seat next to him was Señor Carlos Rojas, the back-up enforcer for the ring.

Then, suddenly, Quintanilla stopped the car, jumped out of the Dodge, jumped into the Ford, and drove away, Carlos Rojas following closely in the Dodge.

It was a fifteen-minute drive across town to 44 Santillane. When they arrived at the clean white cottage, they began unloading the cartons of coke. Inside in the living room was Marcos Osorio, the money courier, and Jorge Vazquez, the other enforcer.

They were just about dropping the cartons to the floor when a swarm of federal narcotics agents hit the cottage. (The only one of the traffickers to escape was Carlos Rojas, who literally threw himself out the window and hasn't been seen or heard from since.)

The next day, Rodriguez and the ring leader were arrested by police and charged with violation of federal narcotics laws.

THE NEW WAY

The cocaine bust I just described, which is really just a Latin version of the French Connection case, today is regarded as an object lesson in how not to smuggle. Not that tremendously large amounts of drugs aren't pushed through from time to time; but it is not the preferred method, and it is not, as far as traffickers are concerned, the method of the future.

The new twist is to saturate the borders rather than ramrod them. The emphasis is on avoiding large, one-shot shipments and instead slipping small amounts through in the hands of large numbers of low-level, unimportant and thoroughly dispensable couriers, known in the business as "mules." The cumulative effect is like that of a constant drizzle as opposed to a squall.

The technique currently in vogue is the courier system. Trafficking organizations recruit large numbers of cheap, relatively desperate people who, for one reason or another, are anxious for a free ride to the States (or Europe) and are willing to do almost anything to get it. These people by and large have no criminal record or previous criminal involvement.

The trafficking organizations in Latin America, for instance, recruit them in:

1. the streets or bars of the major cities. They may even walk up to a stranger and, after feeling him or her out, make an offer. (How would you like to deliver a package to the States for me? I'll give you a free airline ticket and a thousand dollars). In a United States Attorney's office last year, a young prosecutor was looking over a folder prepared by the United States Drug Enforcement Administration. A young woman from Bogotá had been arrested a few nights previous, charged with possession of two kilograms of coke. She had been apprehended at Philadelphia International Airport. Under questioning, she refused to give any information to federal agents other than her name and address. She claimed that she had no idea what was in the package, and had never even heard of a drug called cocaine before. The prosecutor read the agents' report and looked up at me. "This is absolutely typical," he said. "These couriers are like flies. You know, every once in a while we hit one, and maybe we feel like we're doing our job. But what's the impact on the total picture? They just keep sending more and more couriers over. Besides, we'll take her to court, get a conviction and probably the judge will simply deport her. So where are we?"

2. the courtrooms of Latin America. The trafficking people see a woman sitting in court. Her husband or boyfriend is in trouble with the law. The ring offers to put in a good word with the judge ("bribe") in return for the favor of making a trip to the United States to deliver a package to an old friend.

3. the ghettos and slums of the big cities, where any number of desperate people are waiting for Opportunity to knock.

Each year, American law enforcement authorities arrest and deport hundreds of Latin couriers. This represents a fraction of the total. In some instances deported couriers return to the United States the next month through a different port of entry.

Once selected, the courier is outfitted by the ring with (1) a hidden pouch in which the narcotics can be concealed; (2) airline tickets and cash; (3) a phone number to call in New York or Miami or Los Angeles; and (4) a phony passport, possibly.

It is as simple as that.

If and when the courier is stopped, checked and arrested by U. S. Customs agents (and most couriers pass through with no trouble; one Caribbean airline is so notorious for carrying couriers that it is known in some circles as "Air Ganja"), there is really very little the courier can (or will) tell the law. Perhaps the courier really knows nothing more than the first name of the contact who arranged for the trip.

A typical courier routing might start out from Bogotá, stop over in Mexico City (where a phony passport for entry into the United States will be provided by a representative of the ring in Mexico), then on to Montreal. There the courier might rent a car and drive across the Canadian border into Buffalo, where a representative of the ring will arrange for a rendezvous.

Another possibility is that the courier will be provided with a plane ticket from Bogotá to Madrid with a stopover in Miami and New York. The courier will get off the plane in New York, however, for that is the actual destination of the package. The reason for adding "Madrid" is to confuse U.S. Customs officials, who are more conscious of, and concerned with, dope shipments to New York than to Spain (which, after all, is a problem for the Spaniards). Of course, the courier will still have to pass through Customs in New York. But since the passenger was cleared by Customs in Miami, where it was assumed that the passenger was going to Madrid, some of the heat is removed from the courier in New York, where perhaps he will be searched only once. On a flight from Jamaica to the Bahamas last year, I was searched not once but three times by Bahamian customs officials. The reason: my point of debarkation was Jamaica, and I had traveled to the Bahamas via notorious "Air Ganja".

The courier-transit system is quite an improvement over the one-shot-delivery system of a huge amount of narcotics associated with the French Connection method. As in the case of Cuban–Chilean coke case described above, two hundred pounds of cocaine were lost.

But in a courier-transit bust, the loss is negligible in view of the overall volume of traffic moved. Each courier—or "fly," in the words of the United States Attorney—carries only a few keys at most. This new system has revolutionized the smuggling business. U.S. Customs is already besieged with an overwhelming variety of criminal enterprises at their borders. Narcotics isn't the only contraband being smuggled in; among others are stolen art, counterfeit currency, guns.

The criminals have simply found a better way. They usually do. They certainly have a tremendous incentive: money. This is why the criminals are winning the "war on crime."

CHAPTER SEVEN

Team Play

THE TRUCK driver was trembling with fear. He had stopped before
a traffic light on Flatbush Avenue, in Brooklyn, New York, en
route to Long Island, and two *unmasked* gunmen had sprung upon
him and forced him out of the cab and into the back seat of their
own car. In the back seat he had been pushed to the floor and
muffled with a handkerchief over his mouth.

This was bad enough, but what perhaps was most frightening of
all was that the criminals had not even bothered to wear masks.
To the terrified truck driver, there could be only one explanation
for the omission: they planned to kill him, so they hadn't bothered
to disguise themselves.

In one sense this truck driver's concern mirrored the inaccurate
press professional criminals receive in the United States. The
picture that is drawn is one of wild, irrational gunmen who will
kill for a pint of whiskey and who wear grotesque masks on every
run.*

The fact is that truck hijacking is a profitable, rational and far
from bloody business, and the truck driver had no reason to fear
for his life. The criminals were hijackers, not murderers.

* In one respect the press is doing the professional criminal a favor. The
vivid picture of a trigger-happy profession is helpful to the intimidation of
the victim, a process that begins with newspaper accounts of gangland slay-
ings and ends with the drawing of the pistols and the transformation of the
victim into an utter marshmallow.

Truck hijacking is an important crime business. In the New York area alone it is roughly a four-million-dollar-a-year trade. The national average for the net worth of each truck hijack was $47,000. This figure is roughly ten times the national average take of a bank robbery.

It is not only a lucrative crime; it is also a smart crime. In New York State there is not even a specific crime identified as hijacking, even though it is a major underworld business. "There is no formal charge of hijacking in the penal code," says Captain Paul Herny of the Safe, Loft and Truck Squad of the New York Police Department, "so cases become quite involved. We have to charge a man with either kidnapping, robbery or possession of a gun. . . . The charge we get to stick most successfully is criminal possession of stolen property. But then we have a problem proving how a certain carton of cigarettes is actually stolen, or whether the man knew he had stolen property in his possession."

What happens to hijackers who are caught—and most are not—is truly astonishing. In New York State, 99.5 percent of hijacking arrests resulted in dismissed charges, fines or probation. During one year in New York, there were 6,400 arrests for criminal possession of stolen property (the closest the penal code gets to hijacking), and a grand total of *thirty* suspects actually were required to serve time. In one absolutely typical case, eight criminals were arrested and convicted for the criminal possession of women's clothing (they were hijackers). The disposition of the case was that each defendant was fined $2,500 and placed on probation.

This is why I say the truck driver has little to worry about. Judging from these statistics, the average hijacker must know exactly what he is doing. Let's return to the act itself to underscore the point.

There were four men on this team. Two of them had jumped out of the "tail car," as it is called, when the truck had stopped for a light on a deserted stretch of a road one early winter morning a few years ago. The other two stayed in the tail car.

It is usually a simple matter to persuade a truck driver that his life is worth more than the cargo in his truck, and this instance was no exception.

The criminals forced the driver into the back seat of the tail car, gagged his mouth with a large handkerchief, and continued to hold a gun to his head. At the same time, the other gunmen got behind the wheel of the truck and drove it away.

Finally the gunman in the back seat spoke. He told the truck driver that there was really nothing to be afraid of. "This is just a business with us," the truck driver recalled the gunman saying; "no one ever gets hurt on these things."

The driver corrected his partner. He reminded him that once a truck driver had given them a hard time and had to be subdued with a gun butt on the head. His partner said yes, he now remembered that one, but that he was sure this driver wasn't going to give them a hard time, that he realized they were just trying to make a living.

The truck driver couldn't have agreed more.

Then the gunman in the back seat lifted the driver's wallet from his open back pants pocket. He told him that he was opening the wallet to extract the driver's license. A New York driver's license comes in two parts. One is the actual license, the other a renewal stub which is used to obtain a new license upon expiration of the old one.

The gunman told the truck driver that he was taking the renewal stub and placing it in his own wallet. He explained that he was keeping the stub for seven years. After seven years, he said, the statute of limitations on hijacking runs out, and he'd throw the stub away. But if the police ever call on him about this affair, then he, the crazy gunman, is going to go to the residence listed on this renewal stub and empty his gun at the occupants. The only way the cops will ever be able to crack this case, the gunman added, is on the testimony of the only eyewitness.

Did the truck driver understand? A muffled grunt of assent came from the floor of the car. "Okay, fine," said the gunman, "as long as we understand one another, Now, one more thing: when you report this hijacking to the police, tell them the perpetrators were four black males with masks." (The gunman in the back seat and his three accomplices were all Italian-Americans and members of a major New York crime family.)

"Finally," said the gunman, "we have one other request: don't call your boss until you get to South Carolina. This will give us enough time to dispose of the hijacked goods and hide out for a few days."

The truck driver was puzzled. Why South Carolina?

The question was soon answered as the tail car pulled up to La Guardia Airport. The two gunmen and the truck driver got out, and the gunmen pointed him inside, to a booth of Allegheny Airlines. There the gunman purchased a round-trip ticket to South Carolina and gave it to their victim. They took him to the Allegheny gate and put him on the plane. They wished him well, reminded him not to call his boss at the trucking company until after the plane landed, reminded the driver of the license stub which one of the gunmen was holding onto for seven years, and wished him good luck. One gunman even apologized for the inconvenience and, just as the victim was entering the boarding area, gave him a twenty-dollar bill. "After you call your boss," one of them said, according to the truck driver, "go out and have a few on us."

This was classic hijacking at its best. By the time the driver got back to La Guardia on the return flight, he was rather in high spirits, and more than willing to go along with the gunman's request to tell the police a phony story. He had not been physically harmed and, after all, his boss's insurance company would eventually foot the bill for the hijacked cargo. When he had called his boss from South Carolina, his boss, after recovering from the fact that his employee was so remotely located, told the driver not to worry, no one was hurt, and the cargo was insured.

This is the American way of hijacking as practiced by professionals. No one gets hurt, the stolen goods are insured, it's business. It is obvious, even to the most horrified observer, that this system of hijacking has its advantages over one in which the driver is seriously injured or even murdered.

The story that the driver told the police was not entirely convincing, but the cops, familiar with the M. O. ("method of operation") of professional hijackers, knew what the driver was up against, and even sympathized with what, strictly speaking, was tantamount to an obstruction of justice by the driver.

The cops went through the motions of having the victim leaf through a folder of mug shots, but the driver recognized no one.

"Can you blame him?" one cop said, candidly.

Criminals who hijack trucks tend to be professional members of a formal, organized-crime group. Those who are not tend to be what police call cowboys. These are free-lancers, who work hit-and-miss. They will ambush a truck at random without any preparation whatsoever, without even knowing, possibly, what's in the load. On a nationwide scale, these cowboys probably account for a small percentage of the hijackings.

All hijackings require team effort. Usually the team is from three to five men strong. I say *men* because one hears of few females in this business.

Hijacking requires a high degree of organization. In addition to the teamwork of the jacks themselves, there is required the instant cooperation of receivers, or fences. The hijacked goods must move rapidly from hijackers to receivers in order to minimize the possibility of police detection. Usually the hijacking team has already sold the load to a receiver or fence before the truck is hit.

The truck is rarely chosen at random. Sometimes it is offered up by a professional tipster, who may receive up to five thousand dollars for his information. The tipster works for professional criminals, though he usually is not one himself, in the sense of taking an active part in the profession. In the business of crime, the tipster is known as a finger and may be a dockworker moonlighting on the side; a salaried dispatcher for a trucking company, who is obviously in an ideal position to know the future location and exact contents of a truck; or the owner of a truck-stop diner, who will be familiar with the schedules of drivers (and may even phone a pay phone a few miles down the road to alert the hijackers that the man has finished his coffee and Danish and is on his way).

Five thousand may seem like a lot of money for a tip. It *is* a lot of money. But accurate, timely information is well worth the price, especially if the truckload runs into several hundred thousand dollars in fenced merchandise. The tipster may never actually see the money, however. A great deal of fingering for professional criminals is performed by gamblers who took a beating at the tables in some casino, or backroom card game. In over their head, the finger works off the marker—the gambling debt—by performing this useful service.

Once the target truck is identified and the receiver or fence is lined up, the hijackers prepare for the score (which is called a killing, though in the New York area in recent memory no trucker has been seriously injured by hijackers).

A few preliminary notes:

1. In cities where organized-crime families are powerful, like New York and Chicago, hijacking assignments are controlled by crime chiefs and are handed out much like a politician dealing patronage.

2. If, for any reason, the job seems risky, the hijackers chosen by the boss may even subcontract the job to criminals lower down on the totem pole. They may do so even if the hijacking isn't likely to be risky, if they think they can persuade the lower-downs to perform the job for a song.

3. The tools of the trade are: (a) at least one working handgun; (b) a tail car with stolen, false or otherwise misleading license plates; (c) a truck to transfer the goods to, usually a rented Hertz or Avis; (d) a place (known in the trade as a "drop") to store temporarily the stolen goods.

The hijacking occurs most often in the small hours of the morning. This is when traffic is lightest, police manpower thinnest, and eyewitnesses sound asleep. It is also when most trucks are on the road. (Here again, the rules of procedure are not entirely rational. I once observed—quietly and unobtrusively—a hijacking in New

York that took place in broad daylight, at the noon hour, when the streets were swarming with people out to lunch.)

The hijacking team will wait in their tail car at a deserted intersection. They are certain such-and-such a truck will come by, because (a) they are familiar with truck routes and they know the truck comes by Friday mornings around 2 A.M.; or (b) they have been tipped off by a finger; or (c) they have been informed by the driver, who in fact is in on the deal, and in this case, the hijackers will still go through the motions of holding him up, just to protect the driver in the event of an eyewitness.

The hijackers will stake themselves out along the truck's route, follow the truck until an opportune moment, and intercept the truck at a stop sign or a red light.

The hijackers in the tail car will occupy the truck driver until such time as the other half of the crew has dealt with the goods. Whether the hijackers ultimately pack the driver on a plane out of town, or simply drop him on the side of the road after an appropriate wait, one thing is likely: the driver will not be hurt. If there is bloodshed, it can be attributed to the fact that the driver packed a gun, or to the criminal, whose ignorance of classic hijacking procedures caused the problem.

Two of the hijackers are now in possession of the truck, which presumably contains a load of valuable merchandise. The next chore on their list is to drive the truck to the switch point, where another truck will be waiting. The goods will be unloaded onto this second truck and the hijacked truck simply abandoned at the side of the road (or perhaps driven somewhere else to be dropped; professional hijackers have been known to telephone the company with news of where the truck can be recovered; sometimes, the hijackers will take the truck to a fast-paint shop for a new coloring, then drop the face-lifted truck on a main road. The paint job presumably delays police identification of the truck).

The rented truck, with the goods on board, is driven to the *drop,* which can be anything from a rented warehouse to a barn in the country. The drop provides the hijackers with a place to store the goods until they are transferred to the receiver.

When the receiver is lined up, the hijackers drive the goods to still a third spot, known as the *switch point,* where they are turned over to the receiver or his representative.

Several general rules seem universally obeyed by receivers. For one, the receiver and his representative will never be permitted to set eyes on the drop itself. For another, if the drop is raided by police within an unreasonable period of time of the actual hijack— that is, usually twelve hours—then the receiver pays the hijackers for the shipment, anyway. (This is an underworld rule designed to discourage the receiver, or fence, from setting up the hijackers.) Finally, if, due to no fault whatsoever of the receiver, the final switch is not made within twelve hours, and the drop is raided, the hijackers take the loss.

As for the money, the receiver will probably pay the hijacking team between one third and three fourths of the wholesale (not retail) value of the goods.

Actually, rule number two, relating to the twelve-hour fail-safe arrangement, is a joke. Most hijackers have the merchandise in the hands of the receiver in a matter of hours. Hanging onto hot goods is not considered smart business.

Consider the hijacking of perishable goods. During 1973, for example, some ten trailer trucks carrying fresh shrimp and lobster were hijacked in the New York area. The method of operation was unvarying: three hijackers in a tail car stopped and captured driver and truck directly in front of a refrigeration plant on Manhattan's Lower West Side, or within a few blocks of this plant, the tail car having followed at a short distance.

Shrimp hijacking holds a special fascination in view of the urgency of the fencing problem. But these hijackers had their fence ready and waiting (the incidents occurred at the height of the meat and fish shortage on the East Coast in 1973). Within hours of the hijacking, the shrimp were safely stored in the basement of a major fish market in Queens, New York. This market was owned by a man closely associated with one of the five New York organized-crime families.

The shrimp fence immediately arranged for the shipment of the fish produce to restaurants and bars all over Long Island. These establishments, most of which were *not* organized-crime fronts, paid 10 to 20 percent under regular wholesale prices for the shrimp.

The hijackers were evidently under strict instructions to hijack only shrimp. Once they took a trailer truck which carried, as it turned out, $60,000 worth of beef. It must have been a mistake, because the hijackers, with no beef-fence ready at the waiting, simply abandoned the truck at the side of the road—$60,000 worth of beef and all!

CHAPTER EIGHT

Blood Money

CAN A professional criminal ever be a *legitimate* businessman? What happens when criminals take over a legitimate business? Can a wolf ever become a sheep?

To answer these questions we need to spend a few moments on the subject of tight money, an increasingly important one these days.

When the economy is breezing along and profits are the nation's leading cash crop, professional criminals on all levels are in the chips—just like the rest of us. But when the economy sours, and dollars get scarcer than an honest politician, the criminals have to take in their belt a few notches as well as the rest of us. All, that is, except the man of the hour, the loan shark.

The loan shark is an important figure in American life. Long after Chase Manhattan and the Bank of America have slammed shut their doors to all except the blue-chip customer, the loan shark is still processing applications.

He is not a humanitarian, of course. His interest rates are high (usurious, in a word), his foreclosure period short, his collection procedures out of the ordinary. Still, the loan shark occupies a crucial and in some ways misunderstood position, providing liquidity during times when all other sources of instant money have dried up. Taken as a group, the nation's loan sharks amount to a kind of underground federal reserve system, a secret source of funds for those who otherwise would be cut off from support.

Taken as a criminal industry, loan-sharking is regarded by experts as the second largest source of income for professional criminals affiliated with organized crime gangs. Loan money derives primarily from gambling proceeds—the primary source of income for organized crime figures. The New York State Commission of Investigation once reported that in New York City a few years ago exactly 121 leading criminals affiliated with the city's five crime families were active loan sharks, and that many of them had out on loan at least one million dollars each!

The loan shark is a key figure in the crime profession for one other reason. He is the chief economic lever by which professional criminals wedge their way into legitimate businesses. He is the back door to legitimacy. He is also a key figure because he recruits young criminals, steers heist guys to vulnerable targets, and converts legitimate businessmen to scam artists—as we shall see.

In his business, it is always a seller's market. The loan shark sells money—the most expensive money in the world. The usual interest on a loan from a professional criminal is 20 percent per week. Say I go to a loan shark for a fast one hundred dollars. The interest I pay is twenty dollars per week (this is called "juice" in the Midwest and "vigorish" in the East, or "vig"). This means that until I pay back the original principal, I pay the shark twenty dollars per week every week, for as long as it takes. It may take the rest of my life. No matter; I pay the twenty dollars per week.

Long-term financing is an entirely different matter. A common interest rate on longer-term loans is 1½ percent per week. Let me cite an example. Suppose I am a legitimate businessman, but my hotel-casino in the Caribbean is losing money, and I need a fast two hundred thousand to stave off a creditor. My friend at Chase Manhattan doesn't want to see me any more, so overextended is my credit at the bank; I go to a man who knows a man who has this kind of money. A deal is arranged: I get the two hundred thousand next week, in cash, but I have to pay three thousand dollars of interest per week. This is pure interest. The principal of the loan is untouched. In practice, this means that until I can get together the original principal, I am cutting the loan shark in on a percentage of my business.

If I fall behind on the payments, several things can happen. One is that I will encounter the unpleasantry of criminally affiliated credit collectors. If you have ever had a collection agency representative call you on the phone, or even show up at your front door, you know that it can be a very unsettling experience. Imagine how you would react if the men at the front door looked like heavyweight prizefighters with an ax to grind.

In some ways this is not the most painful collection procedure— at least in the long run. Another option open to the loan shark is extracting not a pound of flesh but a percentage of your business. Rather than foreclosing a loan by terminating a life, the creditor offers to exchange the promissory note for an interest (usually 50 percent) through the back door of the forced partnership. Occasionally one sees the delinquent debtor being roughly treated for demonstration purposes, but the exercise seems almost an anachronism in view of the other, more attractive and profitable options open to the "bank." Today the professionals clearly prefer the quiet rustle of exchanging deed and titles to the crunch of bones and the explosion of gunpowder. "Why beat the guy to death," says one Baltimore loan shark, "when we can beat him for his business?" In this respect the criminal loan sharks are patterning their behavior after legitimate banks, which have traditionally required tangible assets as collateral.

Sophisticated loan-sharking banks are in operation around the country. In one celebrated case in New York, the district attorney, in announcing the indictment of just such a bank, rendered the opinion that the loan sharks "did not even have to use threats against their victims, but operated in such a 'legal' way that they were able to collect their ill-gotten gains without ever having to resort to violence. This is a distinct departure from the 'old' loan sharks who dealt in loans with the threat of a beating, maiming, or even death for those who defaulted."

The ring specialized in making loans to small-businessmen with a cash-flow problem. Unless the applicant had some sort of commercial establishment as collateral, the loan sharks usually showed him the door. The bankers were interested not so much in immediate profit as in eventual infiltration of legitimate businesses.

They set interest rates so high that meeting the obligation was almost an impossible task. But, then again, the debtors had to be desperate in the first place to go to a loan shark. "These sharks were collecting not 20 percent of the loan," said the district attorney, "but in the area of 30 percent or more. The defaulters in this case lost their business to these vultures, whose operations were in the millions of dollars annually . . ."

In one instance the owner of a small grocery store went to the sharks for an immediate loan of fifteen thousand dollars. He was not able to obtain a cent from his bank, because he had already extended himself to the limit of his credit. The loan sharks sympathized with the grocer after hearing of his situation, and recommended taking out a second mortgage on his home. The grocer readily agreed and wound up signing a legal note for twenty thousand dollars, even though he walked out of the loan shark's office with only fifteen thousand in his pocket. The difference was the ring's first-day profit.

Thereafter the grocer paid high interest on the full twenty thousand, and before too long found the payments more than he could handle. Eventually, the grocer found himself with a new business partner. "The ring preyed on every kind of small store and commercial operation in the Bronx," said the district attorney. "The stores included pizza parlors, hero-sandwich shops, dry cleaners, grocery stores—you name it; they had it singled out as a target." The district attorney pointed out that in the event of contested default, the ring was in a position to initiate litigation—actually employ the processes of the law with the document or documents the desperate debtor had signed.

Once seated behind the legitimate front—sandwich shop or used-car lot—the professional criminal goes into action, and the legitimate business ceases being legitimate. The classic method of operation, which is still used today, was practiced to perfection by a criminal named Alan Robert Rosenberg in the fifties. Nothing that he did then has been significantly improved upon since, as the "scam" (as they called Rosenberg and his method of corporate manipulation) remains the most common underworld perversion of a once sound business undermined by criminal infiltration.

Rosenberg, who was born in Detroit in 1930, worked with some of the leading criminals in Chicago—including Irwin (Pinky) Davis and Phil (Milwaukee Phil) Alderisio—in perfecting the scheme. Under Rosenberg's shrewd stewardship, the Chicago outfit exploited hundreds of Chicago businesses with hardly a mention of their success reaching the public through media exposure; and in the process they refined a technique that remains a big money-maker for the underworld's more "white-collar" criminals.

Rosenberg's formula for running a legitimate business for short-term criminal gain employed a knowledge of bankruptcy law and of modern credit practice. Cloaked in respectability, it worked at an accelerated pace, puffing up a modest initial investment into a major financial windfall. In 1967, for example, Rosenberg and his key associates worked their way into a Chicago jewelry firm, a respected and well-established business. (Whether they purchased the firm outright, with cash, or whether the firm went down the drain to them over indebtedness is unclear from the record.)

This firm was perfect for Rosenberg's purposes. It had an excellent credit rating with East Coast wholesalers, and a track record of dealing with a large number of firms on a consignment basis. When a professional criminal comes into control of a legitimate business, his immediate hope is to maintain for some time the respectable reputation of his new acquisition.

His first move is therefore an act of omission. Under ordinary business practice, a new owner informs creditors that the firm is under new management. But under ordinary criminal-business practice, the creditors are deliberately kept in the dark for as long as possible. The success of the "one-step scam,"* as it is known in the trade, depends on the maintenance of the illusion for a considerable period that business is being conducted as usual.

To add to the effect, the criminal seeks to demonstrate competency and expertise in the business he has taken over. In the case of this scam, the business was jewelry, and in this Rosenberg himself played a prominent role in the con game by personally telephoning creditors around the country with an expert *spiel*. When hustling jewelers, he once told a close associate, one must master the use and meaning of a handful of technical terms, such as "points," "feathers" and "claws," and sprinkle them liberally in the "rap," or "sketch," as law-enforcement officers sometimes refer to the con. Whatever the business being taken over, the criminal must fit into the environment by sounding at all times like the respectable businessman involved in the routine. The development of a technical vocabulary, Rosenberg always emphasized, was perhaps the crucial element, because under modern business practice the vast majority of deals tend to be conducted over the telephone, in an atmosphere of mutual trust. Talking a good game was half the battle.

Rosenberg's instructions to his working associates included an admonition that reflected a keen understanding of the modern business mentality. This admonition advised his co-conspirators to conduct business with creditors as tenaciously as possible in order to prompt respect for seriousness as a businessman. This instruction meant that his aides were to haggle over price at every opportunity; then, having talked the creditor down, to appeal to his sense of greed by ordering considerably larger quantities of merchandise on credit than had heretofore been the firm's practice. It was important to combine both techniques, for the absence of

---

* "One-step scam" refers to the take-over of a legitimate business by professional criminals for the purpose of defrauding creditors. The "two-step scam" refers to the creation of an entirely new business by criminals under the cover of a respectable front, and the operation of that business for a certain period of time, before implementation of the fraud phase.

either element might possibly signal to the creditor an intention not to make good on the obligation (when the buyer gives up too easily on price) or an inability to meet the obligation (when the buyer haggles over price, then orders a piddling amount of merchandise). In one meeting with a salesman for a New York jewelry wholesaler, Rosenberg himself argued mercilessly over price, then "accepted" from the salesman on consignment no less than fifty thousand dollars' worth of precious stones. (As former government prosecutor Sheldon Davidson put it, the salesman was young and inexperienced, and the clever Rosenberg "simply ate him up.")

The goal of the criminal is to obtain vast amounts of merchandise on credit, to fence the merchandise immediately, and then within a month or two to fold up shop, leaving the legalities of declaring bankruptcy to a front (or "pencil") and his lawyer. When a criminal gains control over a reputable and prestigious jewelry business, the fold-up date might extend several months beyond the initiation of the scam. This is one very good reason why loan sharks are happy to accept payment for defaulted loans in legitimate business rather than in flesh and blood.

(When the firm is not blue-chip, the criminal may seek to polish the firm's financial image by producing for visiting salesmen phony demonstrations of alleged assets. Everything from stolen stock certificates to forged bank accounts may be presented in the effort to create the illusion of solvency. When a salesman indicates a preference for immediate payment by certified check for the first consignment—"to establish good faith"—Rosenberg's method called for countering the request by immediately doubling the size of the order and promising to pay for both with one check upon receipt of the doubled order. This ploy was grounded on the assumption that the salesman's greed for a larger commission would cancel out the salesman's prudence.)

In less than a month behind a desk at the jewelry firm in downtown Chicago, Rosenberg had fenced roughly one quarter of a million dollars worth of jewelry received on consignment. When the fold-up date struck, Rosenberg left town, and the pencil—a former lawyer with the Internal Revenue Service—was left with the books and the bankruptcy courts.

Dealing with bankruptcy is considerably easier than most people suspect. In fact, to the honest but unlucky businessman, bankruptcy law in the United States is a humanitarian out; it permits the loser to liquidate his meager assets and start out anew. But for the dishonest schemer, for a Rosenberg, the laws provide unconscionable but highly profitable escapes from creditors, who are left holding the markers, as it were.

In court, the pencil throws himself at the mercy of the bankruptcy referee. In the absence of any suggestions of criminality—district attorneys are generally ill-equipped for the investigation and prosecution of this "white-collar" crime—and quite often in the absence of protestations by legal counsel representing the creditors, who are more likely to write the loss off as a business expense than to invest further in representation by expensive attorneys, the bankruptcy referee grants the request without further ado. For his part, the petitioner for bankruptcy is required only to provide the court with a reasonable accounting for the disposition of the merchandise received on credit. The usual ploy is to claim that the merchandise was (1) stolen by burglars and reported to police (the burglary never took place, or if it did burglars were encouraged by the pencil to stage the crime); or (2) sold at a considerable loss as the purchasing department overordered, thus creating a cash-flow problem that could be remedied only through immediate and debilitating conversion of inventory into liquidity. Other arguments include the claim by the petitioner that gambling debts soaked up all profits, and that an extramarital affair, an apartment for the woman, the attendant pleasantries, and so forth, induced the petitioner to a life style considerably beyond his means, and the corporation into default of its creditors.

In the absence of in-depth criminal investigation, the criminal's claims will not likely be challenged in bankruptcy court. Bankruptcy courts do not have the resources to deal with complicated financial frauds; they depend on the integrity of the petitioners to arrive at a just ruling. Obviously, this dependence is ideally exploitable by the professional criminal. He—or his pencil—does not approach the court in good faith. On the contrary, the law is important to him only to the extent to which he can profit by it.

There are several profitable routes the professional criminal can take after taking over a legitimate business. But for the last decade or so, the planned-bankruptcy option has been exceedingly popular, precisely because of the rapidity with which the entire scheme can run its course and the magnitude of the profits involved.

When a professional criminal is put into the driver's seat of a legitimate business, the only people who suffer from the change in ownership are the customers and the creditors.

Infiltration of legitimate businesses has become for the underworld a widely preferred technique for making crime pay. There is hardly a major city or suburb in the United States without its share of businesses secretly controlled by professional criminals (see chart next page).*

The Internal Revenue Service has made studies of the phenomenon. It compiled a list of 113 major organized crime figures in the United States. It concluded that 98 of these criminals were involved in 159 legitimate businesses. It found that one criminal syndicate owned real estate interests valued at three hundred million dollars.

According to the President's Commission on Law Enforcement and the Administration of Justice, "racketeers control nationwide

---

* In the city of New York, organized crime interests control the pornography industry. In this chart, drawn by police intelligence experts, three Mafia families are alleged to be the secret interests behind the city's Times Square peep-shows, peep-films, and obscene magazines. The chart was accurate until recently, when changes occurred in the power structure of the New York underworld (the most notable change was the 1971 assassination attempt on Joseph Columbo, member of one of the three crime families represented here. Columbo was seriously incapacitated by the Columbus Day shooting, and his family's power has suffered).

CRIME PAYS!

ORGANIZED CRIME FAMILIES
Direct Involvement in Obscenity Distribution (wholesale and retail)

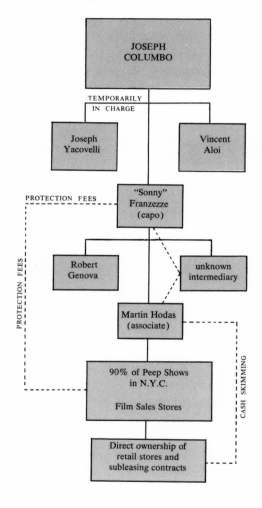

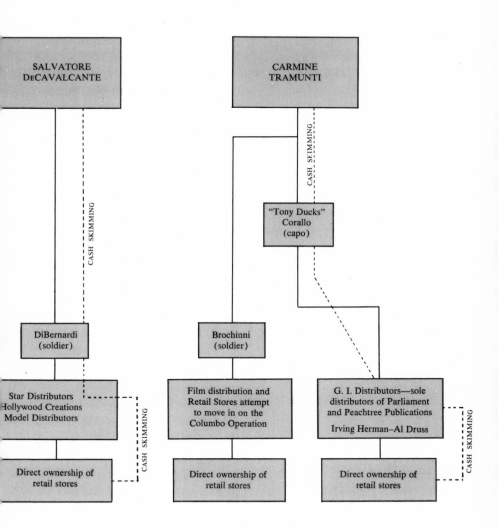

manufacturing and service industries with known and respected brand names." In one Midwestern city alone, it was found that leading racketeers controlled or had large interests in (commonly via loan shark take-overs) 89 businesses with total assets in excess of $800 million and annual income in excess of $900 million.

This is only the beginning. Legitimate businesses are being daily gobbled up by criminal interests. With the possible exception of the U.S. Securities and Exchange Commission, no law enforcement or regulatory agency has been equal to the sophistication of the criminal in this open territory.

The I.R.S. may yet prove the best, last hope in the fight against the bad guys in big business. As long as crime pays, a careful, professional examination of the financial status of suspect corporations will often be revealing. The I.R.S. has yet to move in a comprehensive way against big-time criminals, but the very fact that it has had any success at all holds out some hope for the future.

Another promising law enforcement approach to criminal infiltration of legitimate business is contained in a federal law, Title 18, United States Code, Sections 1961–1964. The heart of the law is the "racketeer-influence and corrupt organizations statute." In law enforcement circles the law is commonly called the RICO statute.

The purpose of RICO is to outlaw the infiltration and illegal acquisition of legitimate economic enterprises and the use of legal and illegal enterprises to further criminal activity. The legislative history behind the 1970 act provides:

> The Congress finds that (1) organized crime in the United States is a highly sophisticated, diversified and widespread activity that annually drains billions of dollars from America's economy . . . (3) this money and power are increasingly used to infiltrate and corrupt legitimate business . . . (4) organized crime activities in the United States weaken the stability of the nation's economic system, harm innocent investors and competing organizations, interfere with free competition, seriously burden interstate and foreign commerce.

A key passage in the law reads:

> It shall be unlawful for *any person* who has received *any income* derived, directly or indirectly, from a *pattern of racketeering* activity or through *collection of an unlawful debt* . . . *to use* or *invest,* directly or indirectly, *any part of* such income, *or the proceeds* of such income, in acquisition of *any enterprise* which is engaged in, or the activities of which affect, interstate or foreign commerce. [Emphasis added.]

This is a very broad law. The bottom line is that it prohibits the reinvestment of illegally acquired money (see a sample reinvestment scheme on the chart on the next page). Other sections of the statute prohibit the illegal acquisition or maintenance of interest or control of any otherwise legitimate corporation; the use of an enterprise to commit illegal acts; and the involvement of a party or parties in any conspiracy to do the above. Among the penalties prescribed by the RICO statute are a maximum term of imprisonment of twenty years and a $25,000 fine for each violation.

Under this law, a man named Milton Parness was convicted in 1970 of one count of acquiring an enterprise through a pattern of racketeering activity. The case is illustrative. In 1967 a successful Pennsylvania businessman invested in the St. Maarten Isle Hotel Corporation, which owned an insolvent and partly completed hotel-casino complex on the Island of St. Maarten in the Netherlands Antilles. By 1970 the legitimate businessman owned about 90 percent of the hotel corporation's stock and had completed the construction of the hotel-casino.

However, the hotel began to lose money, largely because of a Caribbean-wide downturn in the tourist business. In desperation, the businessman arranged for a loan of one hundred and fifty thousand dollars from a New York financier. At the same time, a man named Milton Parness approached the businessman and proposed to solve his and his corporation's financial problems in a single stroke. He persuaded the Pennsylvania man to award him a monopoly on the conduct of junkets to the hotel's casino.

It soon became apparent that the hotel's solvency depended almost entirely upon additional income from gambling junkets to the casino. Each junket participant prior to his departure from the United States was required to deposit gambling "front money" with the junketeer. At the casino in St. Maarten, if his losses at the casino exceeded his initial stake (the usual pattern), he was permitted to gamble on credit. These credit advances were evidenced by signed IOU's, known in the business as "markers." When a player was unable to recoup his losses and thereby redeem his

---

FLOW CHART: THE CRIMINAL MONEY GAME

Start
Invest $2 million in heroin and coke from Latin America

Stop One (two months later) Realize $6 million in profits after drugs are "cut" and sold on street

Stop Two (six months later) Loan-shark $6 million to debt-burdened businessmen in New York, Chicago and Boston; realize $12 million

Stop Three (six months later) Invest $12 million in XYZ Corp. in Caribbean; actually, firm is a shell, and is used only to launder criminal money.

Stop Seven (month later) Take $2 million and . . .

Stop Six (three months later) Skim $2 million off the top of casino earnings, and ship to U.S. in air-freight pouch in non-U.S. airline (so Customs officials can't inspect)

Stop Five (month later) Use $12 million in Miami banks to purchase controlling interest in a Caribbean casino

Stop Four (three months later) Deposit money from XYZ Corp. in various Miami banks; $12 million is now cleansed of its loan-sharking and narcotics origin*

Time Elapsed: 21 months
Total Gain: One Caribbean casino
Overhead Cost: $0.00

* If the bank is not directly owned by the criminals, the laundering fee is 10 percent, or, in this case, $1.2 million.

markers prior to his return to the United States, it was the responsibility of the junket manager to collect such debts and to forward them (minus a commission) to the hotel. (The junket manager was also responsible for forwarding the front money to the hotel.)

By the fall of 1970 Parness, who was solely responsible for the marker collection and the forwarding of front money, had found out about the $150,000 loan. In late 1970, the New York businessman began pressing the hotel owner. The owner in turn repeatedly asked Parness for approximately $400,000 in overdue marker receivables which Parness claimed he had not yet been able to collect.

The truth was that Parness was holding back on the hotel owner as part of a grand scheme to gain control of the hotel. As the New York businessman was about to foreclose on the loan (and thereby gain controlling interest in the hotel, the collateral that was put up), Parness suddenly offered to arrange for the hotel owner to get $150,000 in the form of a loan from "some friends."

Actually, these friends were simply fronts for Parness, and the money that was lent to the hotel owner was none other than the marker money that Parness had in fact collected but was holding back from the Pennsylvania businessman.

During February and March of 1971, the Pennsylvania businessman remained unsuccessful in his efforts to get the marker receipts from Parness. At the same time, and by no concidence whatsoever, Parness' friends prepared to exercise their foreclosure rights under the businessman's pledge of stock to the hotel-casino. By April 3, after various legal maneuverings, the businessman was formally divested of his 226,500 shares of hotel-casino stock.

The scheme was finally halted by the U.S. Justice Department's Strike Force 18, which prosecuted the RICO statute. Strike Force investigators had uncovered the vicious plot, and Parness was brought to trial, and convicted, under the RICO statute.*

---

* There is one other aspect of the RICO statute worth mentioning. Section 1964(a) of Title 18 grants the district courts power to hear civil action by the United States to stop criminal syndicates and businesses without having

The Parness case is absolutely typical of the methods employed by professional criminals to obtain control of perfectly legitimate businesses. What was untypical in this case was that the criminal was stopped in his tracks by vigorous law enforcement. For every successful Parness prosecution, untold others go undetected and unprosecuted.

The volume of the activity is simply overwhelming. In the area of planned bankruptcy alone, according to a study by the United States Chamber of Commerce, more than a thousand uninvestigated scams are pulled off annually—and some 250 of them are perpetrated by high-ranking criminals, each scam involving up to 250 or more creditors and upwards of $250,000 in merchandise or currency. One veteran investigator insists that in criminally motivated scams the minimum amount of money involved is one hundred thousand dollars.

---

to first prove criminal violations. The little-known section was invoked with great success in Chicago in 1974 by federal strike-force attorneys. The government went to court to seek an injunction against seven men accused of running a bookmaking operation from an establishment called Western Avenue Billiards, a pool hall. The judge issued the injunction (and the Seventh U.S. Court of Appeals upheld the injunction), enjoining the defendants from placing, receiving or collecting bets. The government also asked the court that all seven defendants in the criminal action submit to the U.S. Attorney in Chicago quarterly reports for the next ten years revealing all sources of personal income (failure to do so would lead to a contempt-of-court citation). Elements of the case, at this writing, have been appealed to the Supreme Court, but federal prosecutors are hopeful that the statute will remain on the books, allowing them to hamper criminal operations without having to prove in criminal court an actual criminal violation. The civil suit approach to dealing with profitable criminality is an entirely new area that has not yet been fully exploited.

CHAPTER NINE

Bad Guys

"If they can get Meyer, they can get anybody."
                              —A New York criminal

"They'll never get Meyer."
                    —A Miami criminal attorney

TO PROFESSIONAL criminals, it was almost like the famous Dreyfus case.

On the face of it, of course, the comparison may seem a little ridiculous. Still, from the criminal perspective, it was a political trial. It occurred in 1973, when the executive branch of the government was secretly engaged in shocking acts of domestic surveillance and obstruction of justice. It came at a time when the Nixon administration's much-vaunted law-and-order campaign had come to a screeching halt behind miles of hypocrisy, deception and outright ineptitude, under Attorney General John N. Mitchell. To make up for all its mistakes and deceits, the Nixon administration launched an all-out war on one seventy-two-year-old man, who, as it happened, was also a Jew. In short, it came at a time when the good guys weren't much better than the bad guys. The trial was seen as an attempt to resurrect for the consumption of the public the boundaries between the two.

This is the criminal perspective on the 1973 trial of Meyer Lansky, the reputed chairman of the board of organized crime in the United States. The occupancy by Lansky, the multimillionaire crime boss, of a seat behind the defense table under these circumstances was viewed by many professional criminals as evidence of frustration and hypocrisy by a government whose decades of overall ineptitude had been exceedingly instrumental in the rise of a professional criminal class in the United States.

It was not necessary to remind criminals, after all, that, while Meyer Lansky was over the years efficiently gluing together his estimated three-hundred-million-dollar empire from the rackets, the federal government was denying the very existence of organized crime, and that, while Lucky Luciano, Frank Costello and Joseph Bonanno were modernizing and expanding the modern Mafia, the FBI and the late J. Edgar Hoover were persistently arguing that the Honored Society was no more than the fictional creation of a handful of newspapermen with overwrought imaginations, and that, while professional criminals of all ethnic backgrounds were stringing together vast networks of vice, narcotics, sharking, gambling, real estate ventures and so on, federal agents were racing around the country at considerable expense to the taxpayer (in more ways than one) snuffing out the headline criminals, the Bonnies and Clydes, the inconsequential bank robbers and penitentiary escapees and minor dope peddlers, who in absolute dollar value amounted to perhaps and at best one day of interest in a single slow business day in the life of Meyer Lansky.

The man was a giant. His trial was an historic confrontation between the so-called law, on the one hand, and the lawless, on the other.

Yet, at the same time, there was something downright laughable about the proceeding. Perhaps it was the charge—that of having evaded taxes on, and concealed from the government, sums amounting to less than one hundred thousand dollars. To you or me, perhaps, this may seem like a lot of money. But to Meyer Lansky, if all estimates of his personal wealth are anywhere close to the mark, this is walking-around money.

On top of this, Lansky was troubled by a heart ailment. Had he been in perfect health, perhaps the trial would have been regarded as nothing more than ritual dues-paying to which professional criminals are well accustomed. The principals in a criminal justice system, after all, must occasionally have their day in court, and for the prosecutors—the youthful government attorneys R. J. Campbell and John Dowd—and the prominent and prosperous Miami defense counsel E. David Rosen, the exercise no doubt had its rewards.

Lansky, of course, had known what was coming well before presentation of the indictment by a federal grand jury. The previous year he had fled to Israel in search of permanent citizenship and, thus, some protection from extradition to the United States. This move was occasioned not so much by fear of conviction and imprisonment as by the wish to avoid hassle and risks to health, which for Lansky in the past few years had become a very real concern. But the Israeli government of Golda Meir, backed by the Israeli Supreme Court, and both under severe pressure from Washington, denied the application for citizenship, thus setting the stage for the extraordinary 1973 trial of the nation's leading professional criminal.

The trial was closely watched by criminals for other reasons. Income tax indictments have proven the government's most effective weapon against successful criminals, from the days of Al Capone to the present, and there was some slight tremor of concern in underworld circles about the outcome. This piqued interest stemmed not so much from a gush of sympathy for a racketeer emeritus like Lansky, stuffed into the docket and on the verge of a physical breakdown, but from a professional interest in significant developments on the law-and-order front. As one New York criminal put it, "If they can get Meyer, they can get anybody."

The statement was a tribute to the crime boss's remarkable facility for evading not only income taxes but the punitive power of the penal code, over the course of a career that stretches from Prohibition to the current epoch of professional criminals, with their hotels, casinos and real estate transactions, masquerading as legitimate businessmen (see chart below).

In this sense, perhaps the federal government had every right in the world to nail Meyer Lansky in any way it could. After all, what he had done over the years was not at issue; the difficulty was in proving each and every—or even one!—allegation. To honest, hard-working prosecutors in the federal government (and there are some), the income tax indictment was simply the best they could do under the circumstances.

THE ROAD TO BECOMING CHAIRMAN OF THE BOARD: THE ARREST RECORD OF MEYER LANSKY
Born: Grodno, Russia, 1902
Name: Maier Suchowljansky

1. October 24, 1918	Manhattan. Felonious assault. Disposition: discharged after pleading guilty to disorderly conduct
2. November 14, 1918	Manhattan. Disorderly conduct. Dis: $2 fine
3. August 16, 1920	Manhattan. Disorderly conduct. Dis: $2 fine
4. March 6, 1928	Queens (N.Y.). Felonious assault. Dis: charges dismissed by judge
5. March 7, 1928	Manhattan. Homicide: Dis: dismissed by judge
6. January 6, 1929	Manhattan. Possession dangerous drugs (Public Law 1752). Dis: discharged by judge
7. November 23, 1931	Brooklyn (arrested under alias of Morris Lieberman) Violation of Volstead Act (smuggling liquor). Dis: convicted, $100 fine
8. April 19, 1932	Chicago. Held as suspect. No charge, released
9. September 10, 1952	New York State Police. Charge: conspiracy, common gambler; forgery, 3rd degree. Dis: released on $10,000 bail
10. May 2, 1953	On previous charge, convicted as common gambler, sentenced to three months in county jail and $2,500 fine

11. February 11, 1958	Manhattan. Vagrancy (no visible means of support). Discharged 2/27/58 after being held for sixteen days
12. August 20, 1958	Broward County, Florida. Operating a gambling house from November 1, 1948, to February 21, 1950 (Green Acres Club, Hallendale, Florida). Agreed to plead guilty to Grand Jury "information." Dis: fined $1,000
13. 1971	Miami. Federal Grand Jury indictments for (1) failure to comply with a grand jury subpoena and (2) conspiracy to defraud the government of the United States (income tax) Dis: on (1) conviction; conviction on appeal; (2) acquittal by jury trial

Total time spent behind bars: three months, sixteen days.

After all, hardly anyone believed that Lansky had retired from the ranks of the criminal world. Even at his advanced age and in failing health, it was reasonable to believe he was still active: elder criminals hardly ever fade away; it is only when they die—often from unnatural causes—that they are absolutely removed from the scene. Besides, as chairman of the board, he was not actually required to pound the pavement or work harder than any other corporate board chairman.

The man's power and influence in American life is such that few could believe that the trial would end in a conviction. As one Miami attorney put it, "They won't get Meyer. They'll never get him."

They did not get Meyer. After a scant afternoon of deliberation, the Miami jury acquitted the defendant on all counts of the indictment. Lansky himself did not even wait for the jury's verdict. Either he was too ill to wait it out, or too confident of the verdict to bother hanging around the federal courtroom in the old post office building in downtown Miami.

When the foreman announced the predictable, Lansky was at his condominium apartment on Collins Avenue in Miami Beach with his wife, Thelma, a former hotel manicurist; and, shortly thereafter, the two young prosecutors returned to Washington, beaten by the man who had so magically eluded the Justice Department for so long.

Was the trial worth the taxpayers' money? Well, yes, and on two counts. First, like the prosecutors from the Justice Department, I believe that it is worth the try, and that it is appropriate to attempt to get a conviction with whatever material is at hand. It was, after all, hardly the fault of the two young U.S. attorneys that Meyer Lansky had not been dumb enough to provide investigators with the kind of evidence and mistakes that are so obvious that even a jury conviction can be obtained. And even if it were possible to gather together in a Miami courtroom a jury of Lansky's peers— and who should sit on that body? Millionaires only? Criminals only? Politicians? Magicians? Financial wizards?—it was not likely that the chairman of the board would allow himself to descend into the lower levels of criminal transaction which the nation's criminal codes are ideally suited to punish.

When he was young, of course, that was a different matter. A stint on the streets, a little burglary, a little car theft. Then a shot at narcotics, into gambling and numbers. Then on up the ladder, bypassing Lucky Luciano (deported), on past Costello (a burnt-out case), on past Bonanno (a shipwrecked godfather), on past Columbo (a human vegetable now, after the 1971 assassination attempt), until he was so high up in the crime world that there were more layers between him and any of the usual levels that government investigators could see from below than rings around a giant redwood.

This was his secret, of course: the layering of the non-Italian godfather from both the legitimate and the criminal worlds. Finding Meyer Lansky within a mile of an indictable offense was to be like finding Caesar's wife hustling on the street. Suspicions, there were plenty of; but hard, indictable evidence was a different matter entirely.

Still, the trial had its redeeming moments. One moment came when a Miami neurologist named Dr. Sherif Shafey told the court about the results of a battery of tests he had administered to the defendant.

What an enviable responsibility! It would be possible, I think, to fill Times Square with the multitude of people who would dearly love to administer a battery of intellectual and emotional tests to the chairman of the crime board. But the task was Dr. Shafey's alone.

He delivered a line, one hot summer morning in 1973 in the packed downtown federal courtroom, that completely wrecked, at least for the moment, the solemnity of the proceedings; yet the good doctor himself hardly smiled a whit. Testifying in connection with the test, the doctor said, "He was slow in answering questions in several areas of specific dates, and he could not recall immediate and recent events. . . . But as far as his ability to use figures and calculate numbers was concerned, he was capable of doing well."

The spectators in the courtroom roared with laughter. It was as though Demosthenes had been given, grudgingly, an "A" in remedial speech.

Another high point came with the testimony of Vincent Teresa, an overweight, former ranking member of the New England crime family of Raymond Patriarca. Teresa had been caught red-handed by federal authorities in the middle of a phony stock transaction and, to everyone's surprise, had *sung,* in underworld parlance, like a frightened canary.

He performed one of his better numbers at Lansky's trial. He testified that he knew Lansky through his associates in the mob, and that he had even met the master on two occasions when he was in Miami to deliver *skim* money from a London casino.*

---

* "Skim" is a term used in reference to casino profits which are not reported to the appropriate governmental authority as taxable income. For example, if a casino takes in two hundred thousand dollars in a night of gambling, it may report to the tax authority, say, one hundred and fifty thousand and simply skim off the rest (like cream risen to the top) to the casino's backers. In this case before the federal jury here described, it was alleged that Meyer Lansky was a recipient of the London casino's skim. In the last decade, skim money from junkets to Las Vegas and the Caribbean has grown enormously as a source of income for leading professional criminals.

On one occasion, he testified, he handed the defendant thirty thousand dollars in cash in an office at the Dupont Plaza Hotel in downtown Miami. As Teresa spoke to the packed courtroom, a perceptible tone of awe crept into his voice. For Teresa was not only the highest-ranking mobster ever to turn government witness to date (much higher than Valachi, a mere soldier), but he was also the first ever to testify against Lansky, which in some circles is tantamount to signing one's own death warrant. (Even today, Teresa remains in seclusion, having been given a new identity and a new geography by the federal government as a reward for his testimony not only in the Lansky case but in roughly two dozen others.) Teresa knew that his was a rare performance.

On the first occasion, he said, he gave the money to either Lansky or an associate of the master's in the office in Miami. Somehow, Lansky wound up with the money. Teresa was asked by the prosecutors what Lansky did with the money.

Said Teresa, "He just laid it on the desk and was just moving it around like you'd move a pack of cigarettes."

Then there was a second meeting. This time Teresa brought down from New England, after another successful junket to London, fifty thousand in cash. What happened this time?

"Mr. Lansky just laid it on the table," the mobster said, "and thumbed through it."

The jury was moved to an acquittal—not surprisingly. After all, the chief witness against the defendant—Vincent Teresa—was more unsavory-looking than the defendant himself.* This of course is the cross government prosecutors must bear in trials against organized-crime figures. Usually the only way to get at a big shot is to put on the stand an underling who is even less literate and wholesome in appearance than the big shot. Juries, being by and large

---

* Also, Lansky's lawyer—a well-known Miami defense attorney—got Teresa, the government's star witness, to confess that he was a congenital liar! This tended to undermine his previous testimony.

very civilized bodies, are often turned off by the lack of quality of the prosecution's witnesses. They are, perhaps, not to be faulted for wondering whether the witness's testimony is in fact the truth.

Another consideration: Lansky himself played his hand perfectly. The trial had been given such a huge build-up in the Miami papers that it was almost impossible to believe that this short (five-foot-four), quietly dressed man, this frail figure of a gentleman, was everything that the press had made him out to be. He kept his place, and peace, behind the defense table, did not speak unless spoken to, and when he took the stand answered the prosecutors' questions in a low, respectful voice.

He wasn't even dressed that well. He had worn, day after day, dark slacks and a light-blue sports coat. He might have purchased them at any of a dozen retail clothing stores in town. They certainly did not look tailored. And where was the ominous looking tinted sunglasses? Or the pearl-studded cigarette holder? Or even the diamond rings?

Meyer Lansky has been accused of many offenses by police and prosecutors, not to mention journalists, in his lifetime. But the one thing they never accused him of being was dumb. Lansky simply didn't want to look the part.

To the professional criminal, the end of the trial was a fitting tribute to the man they all looked up to. Once again, he had slithered off the hook.

Meyer Lansky is *the* professional. With his all-American wife, Thelma, and two sons (one of whom was graduated from West Point), with his associates in many sectors of legitimate American business (especially the liquor industry), with his vast investments in real estate, resorts, hotels and casinos, both in the United States and abroad, the man comes as close to the perfectly formed mythic figure in American criminal history as has yet come our way. By comparison, the Lucianos, Costellos and Bonannos seem like cheap thugs running two-bit dives.

He is perhaps as important a figure in the context of America's growth into a hugely rich capitalistic society as any number of far more studied phenomena, like John D. Rockefeller or Franklin D. Roosevelt. As the leading practitioner in a gigantic crime profession, this former Brooklyn auto thief remains the unexplored dark side of our souls.

In a way, the jury of Miamians who acquitted Meyer Lansky of charges of evading income tax on less than one hundred thousand dollars between 1967 and 1968 rendered a much larger verdict for the nation. The United States has simply never been able to put him away for good. In that single statement of fact lies the whole history of law enforcement against organized crime boiled down to its essential truth.

Meyer Lansky was not so much the solitary pioneer cowboy crossing brave new frontiers as a true organization man who served an organization that served his interests. He was not one of a kind, but simply the best of the lot. He was a criminal who became a businessman rather than a businessman who became a criminal, and the distinction is crucial. He comes out of a tradition, a body of technical knowledge, a set of attitudes, and a consciousness about the profession which is vintage American criminal.

Mickey Cohen, a former racketeer and associate of Meyer Lansky, comes out of that same tradition. Where Cohen departs from tradition, however, is in his willingness to talk—on tape—about his life in the rackets. Indeed, when Cohen was organizing Meyer Lansky's gambling operations on the West Coast in the forties and fifties, he was a steady source of information for the news media, a candid and voluble individual in a profession not known for its press conferences.

Recently I spent some time with the aging but still articulate Mickey Cohen in his Los Angeles apartment. It seemed to me that as one who had worked on both the lower and higher rungs of the crime ladder, Cohen was uniquely qualified to discourse philosophically about his life work, which he did much as a retiring surgeon might review his fifty years under the operating lights. And as a protégé of Lansky, Cohen might have some sense of where his profession was headed. What follows is a condensed and considerably edited version of our talk.

PLATE: Would you advise a young man—your son, say— to go into the racket world?

MICKEY: If I had a son, I'd say to him, look son, if you've got the makeup and everything in your system to be a boxer —I was in the fight business for seven years, you know—I would say to my son, lookit, if you want to be a boxer, if you want to be in the underworld, in the so-called racket world, I'd say, lookit, it's your choice. . . . If you want to be a boxer, and you see to it that you don't have the makings to be a top boxer, forget about it. If you're going into the so-called racket world, and you don't have the makeup for it, then . . . in other words, as Harry Truman used to say, if you can't take the heat, don't go into the kitchen.

PLATE: But a lot of sons of today's top mobsters don't seem to have it, or don't want it.

MICKEY: That's right. . . . A lot of mistakes were made which brought about, which caused a lot of deaths and a lot of prison sentences and a lot of failures, because certain people labored under the misapprehension that just because Mickey Cohen's son, was Mickey Cohen's son, that made him okay, that made him more of a man than he may have been. Now, Mickey Cohen's son may not have the makeup for that sort of thing. The rule applies everywhere, in other fields. That's what brought about a lot of mistakes in the so-called racket world. What the hell, just because somebody was so- and so's son or so-and so's *gumbar,* didn't make him have the makeup for what they wanted him to be.

PLATE: Like Bill Bonanno [the son of Joseph Bonanno, the former boss of a New York Mafia family]?

MICKEY: Like Bill Bonanno. That's right. You know, I've been away eleven years [in prison], and I've had to catch up on a lot of things. And a lot of sons in later years have come to the decision that they didn't have the makeup for it, and didn't want to follow in their father's footsteps, or in their uncle's footsteps. Take John Tunney, Gene's son . . .

PLATE: The Senator?

MICKEY: Yeah, the Senator. He'd probably, if you ever took a punch at him, he'd probably fall over, just from trying to keep his arms up. It don't automatically make him a great fighter, I'm just using this as an example. This is where many mistakes have been made in the racket world. . . . I'm not trying to speak egotistically—impress you or anything, but this is an argument I made many years back [to Syndicate leaders]. I expressed myself many times and caused great animosity for it.

PLATE: Even in a modern, legitimate corporation, that would be considered bad business.

MICKEY: Right. That's what I'm talking about. You may be a great writer, I don't know. But if you had a son, you might like to have your son become a famous writer, but your son may not have the makeup for it. That's what happened to the sons of great actors here in Hollywood—like Edward G. Robinson's son. . . . It's hard when you have to follow up on something when you just don't have the makeup for it.

PLATE: There's a lot of speculation today that with blacks and Latins moving into the crime world, there's been a radical change in the makeup of the American underworld. Do you see such a radical change taking place?

MICKEY: None whatsoever. There have been some stories about how people back East tried to bring some colored people into positions—now I don't mean this as a bigot—but the makings of the so-called syndicate, the racket world— back in the days of Owney Madden, Dutch Schultz, Lucky Luciano, these were people who were born for it. You just don't make somebody. . . . You can't make a person, you just can't make a racehorse out of a mule and that's the whole story.

PLATE: Are there any young people coming up who are promising?

MICKEY: To be honest with you, I found one man, in all the time I've been home, that I would even consider a possibility.

PLATE: What qualities would it take, to live that kind of life?

MICKEY: One of the strongest is faithfulness. You know, I have this trouble with my sister. She just doesn't understand it. Once she was robbed, and so she called me up, asks whether she should call the police. I say for Chrisakes, go call the cops. I tried to explain it to her. She wasn't in the so-called racket world, so of course she should. Now, if that happened to me or to someone else in our world, why then it's a different thing. That's what I mean by faithfulness. . . . And naturally, you've got to have guts. Guts that the ordinary person would look upon as being crazy. . . . You have to have strong standards personally. Now, I'm no angel, but in my way of life, I've lived up to my ethics. . . . Loyalty, that's the strongest thing. If a man is *right,* if a man doesn't pass himself off, you know what I mean? Let me explain to you. If you walk outside this door and get stuck up, it's right for you to automatically call the police. But if it happens to me, or to him [gesturing toward his valet Jimmy Smith] it's not right. That's the difference.

PLATE: An absolute, clear demarcation between the two worlds?

MICKEY: That's right. I'm talking about a guy being a stool pigeon. The stool pigeon is a son of a bitch, he portrays himself as a tough guy, a right guy.

PLATE: In New York City today, and in other cities, I would say that there are more police informants than you can count.

MICKEY: That's right, that's right. Don't forget, I'm not operating any more, but I know most of the people in this business in the country and probably around the world.

PLATE: It's often said that what the racket world does is to give people what they want but are unwilling to publicly admit they want.

MICKEY: No question about it, no question about it. The racket world couldn't exist for five minutes without outside people. I couldn't have lasted five minutes if I didn't have partners in every officialdom, in every high office where it was necessary to have cooperation. Not five minutes! Three minutes! Nothing! How else are you going to exist? . . . Now we used to have a sheriff here, a finer old man never existed, believe me. Probably a lot of people would say he was politically dishonest. But he was a *tremendously* honest person. . . . This sheriff as powerful as he was, each four years that he had to go for office, to make sure he would win without

a runoff, there had to be $400,000. Now, when you find out
the kind of money it takes to get into office. . . . Take our
Presidency. It pays, what is it, two hundred thousand dollars
a year, right? Now it takes anywhere from seventy-five to
one hundred million dollars to become President. Let's use
common sense, and it's a wonder that the public doesn't use
common sense more. Now, why would a man who's going to
have to raise seventy-five to one hundred million dollars a
year be willing to take a job that's going to pay two hundred
thousand dollars a year? Use common sense. . . . Now I'm
only using this as one example. Now, this goes for one office
right on up the other. Now, you can't get in office today, I
don't care who you are, without money.

PLATE: Now Mr. Smith was saying, as I came in earlier,
that as it will apparently come out in your autobiography,
you contributed heavily to some of Richard Nixon's cam-
paigns. Is this true?

MICKEY: Exactly right. If somebody ever told me that
Richard Nixon would have been President of the United
States when I first met him [when he was running for the
House of Representatives in 1946] it would be the same
thing as if somebody said to me, you see this guy Tom
Plate, he's going to be President of the United States in ten
years. I would have more believed it of you. This guy [Nixon]
was like a ward heeler, a nickel-and-dime politician . . . You
know, when they say truth is stranger than fiction, believe
me, there's no bigger truth than that.

PLATE: How do you feel when you see some politician to
whom you've given money, on the stump denouncing crime
and gangsters in the United States? How do you feel about
these hypocritic sermons?

MICKEY: Hah, hah. I had a man, a politician, I used to
drive him to the television station to make his speech, and I'm
sitting in the Green Room, waiting for him to finish to go to
dinner with him, I'm paying for the campaign, I brought him
to this broadcast, and I'm listening to him on television, right
here in the next room, and here he says, I assure you citizens
of the county of Los Angeles that the first thing I'll do if
elected is to rid Los Angeles of the likes of Mr. Cohen and
his ilk, or words to that effect. And it's very important for me
for this guy to get into office, so I'm happy for every word

he says. But the public eats this stuff up. . . . Now, once Nixon gets up in front of a crowd of people, I threw a banquet for Nixon, with Murray Chotiner—remember Murray Chotiner?—now there wasn't one legitimate person at this dinner. And Nixon got up to speak. Now this is the fact of political life.

PLATE: A similar way of looking at policemen would be possible, too?

MICKEY: Right, Absolutely. I have some policemen still with me today that were with me for twenty-five or thirty years. Old-timers. Of course, some of them are retired. We sit here and talk, they come here and seek me out. There's hardly a day goes by that I don't get a call from them. In the true sense of the word, they were dishonest policemen, but actually they were as honest as the day was long. Now they wouldn't pinch you for some poker game in your house, for some nickel-and-dime bullshit thing, excuse my language. These were policemen who cleared up many and many a crime in this city. I respect them to the hilt. There was a time I was known in the newspapers as a cop-hater, a cop-fighter. But actually this was the furthest thing from the truth.

PLATE: What was your relationship with newspaper men? You seemed to have a flair there.

MICKEY: One time I was driving home from a day in court. In the car with me was a newspaper editor. I was taking him to my home for dinner. It's about five-thirty, that's when his newspaper came out, and we stop to pick up a copy of the paper. His wife was already at home with my wife, they had played golf together that day. . . . Now there's this headline on the paper that night, and the headline is as completely untrue as it could be, as if somebody said you and I are sitting here now playing poker. Now I say to Jim, why you dirty son of a gun, how can you print something like that? And he says to me, for Chrisakes, Mick, when are you going to wise up? Don't you know, when we ain't got news, we're going to use something that's going to sell papers, even if we have to use your name. Wouldn't you do the same thing, if you were head of the paper? And I had no answer to that.

PLATE: When you were in the rackets, did you feel that in some sense you were really part of what was making this country go, that you were not freaks or strangers, but somehow vital elements in the society?

MICKEY: Yes, and this is what bothers me now, I resent that in the so-called racket world today, it's become a place for freaks.

PLATE: What directions will the racket world take in the years to come?

MICKEY: Well, for years people in the racket world have been drawing further and further from prostitution. As much as they possibly could. And there was only a lower ilk of the underworld that had anything to do with it, anyway. And in the last fifteen years narcotics has become an absolute no-no, anything to do with narcotics whatsoever. I'm talking now about the *true* people in the underworld. And now they've drawn away from counterfeiting. That's the belief of the top persons with knowledgeable minds, that's the thinking. That's the way to stay out from under the government's feet.

PLATE: In other words, there are some things you can do with a reasonable degree of security, and there are other things that are too much of an affront to the authorities.

MICKEY: That's right. If you go into anything that has to do with counterfeiting, for example, you have to contend with the Secret Service, not to mention the FBI and everyone else, you understand?

PLATE: So you have to be absolutely crazy to get into this stuff?

MICKEY: Absolutely crazy, you have to be. Particularly in anything where you have to deal with more than one person. If it's just one person, you've got a chance, especially in a field like gambling, which is looked upon in a somewhat favorable light. But narcotics. You ain't got chance one, you're a goddam fool.

PLATE: Especially with all the informants running around.

MICKEY: That's right.

PLATE: What did you think of the Meyer Lansky trial, you know, the one in 1973 in Miami when he was tried on income tax? Some people I know back in New York were very annoyed at the Justice Department for bringing up a seventy-two-year-old man and dragging him up for trial at this point. What do you think?

MICKEY: No question, no question. I'm not so goddam angry at this country, this country was just using it as a means for covering up a lot of bullshit that was going on with Nixon politically. They used him for publicity. But I'm angry with Israel, with Golda Meir, and all those other bullshits.

PLATE: So there was a tremendous amount of hypocrisy?

MICKEY: Oh, the worst in the world. Only a Jew could have deported him. [Lansky had sought citizenship in Israel in 1972.] And it ain't easy for me to say that. And I told that to Golda Meir, I sent her a letter. This was a disgrace to all Jewdom.

PLATE: What's your impression of Lansky?

MICKEY: He's a decent human being. Very shrewd human being. A decent man. . . . He's done good for everybody. He may have done a few bad things as a youngster, but we all have. I've done some things in my day, I have to pinch myself today to believe I actually did them. We all go through different things. But since then, he's become a diplomat and a humanitarian of the highest caliber.

PLATE: So today, he's considered an elder statesman of the racket world?

MICKEY: Of any world, not just the racket world, he's an elder statesman as a person. Like Barney Baruch, in New York, when he was an elder statesman, you went to him for advice. That's Meyer Lansky today. . . . Now, after what Israel did to him in not granting him citizenship I don't give a goddam what happens to them. Do you have any idea, Tom, what I sent back to that country? I sent them arms we never got to use in this country, in the Second World War. Anything we could get our hands on we sent back to Israel. I'm not taking all the credit now. Guys like Al Anastasia helped. So what did they do? They showed the lowest, yellow-belly of any race of people in the world. What is Israel? It's supposed to be a refuge for any Jew that's looking for a place to live. He wasn't even a lamster when he went, he wasn't even indicted. So what did they do? What right did they have to throw him out of there, those rotten, dirty sons-of-bitches?

PLATE: And why do you think the Justice Department indicted him?

MICKEY: Anyone with common sense can figure that one out. Only to show they're after crime, just a bullshit thing. . . . And then he was acquitted!

PLATE: You obviously have a great deal of admiration for

Mr. Lansky. Do you see anyone in the business now who is likely to be the Meyer Lansky of the future?

MICKEY: To tell the truth, no. I don't see nobody like that.

Perhaps the most significant change in the crime world since Cohen's heyday in the forties and fifties has been the growing criminalization of labor unions in the United States. In many labor locals, professional criminals hold important executive positions. Many of these "executives" have criminal records and extensive experience in the racket world, from auto theft to loan-sharking and extortion. Union locals in twenty-five different sectors of business and industry, according to the United States Chamber of Commerce, are under the tight control of professional criminals.

The Enemy Within, a study by the late Robert F. Kennedy, brought out the intensive involvement of criminals in the affairs of the Teamsters' Union. Today, more than a decade after the book was published, the close working relationship between top union officials and professional criminals is now not even discreet. It is my guess that the Meyer Lansky of the eighties will arise out of criminally corrupt labor unions.

Certainly, the corruption of the labor movement represents the most significant advance for organized crime in this latter half of the twentieth century. It has given professional criminals a firm toehold in American politics, labor unions being a major electoral and legislative force, and has contributed mightily to the atmosphere of corruption that absolutely stifles the political processes of American cities. On top of this, labor unions, with their pension funds held in trust, provide, under criminal management, instant access to impressive amounts of liquidity, which can be loan-sharked to cash-starved businesses, or secretly invested in real-estate ventures owned by criminals and/or their collaborators. Union welfare and pension funds amount to approximately $100-billion, and are expanding rapidly. They are the professional criminal's prime target for exploitation.

One of the rare law enforcement successes against this sort of white-collar fraud was achieved by federal prosecutors in Chicago in 1973. A federal grand jury indicted seven persons in connection with gross misuse of pension funds. The indictment charged that two of the defendants had received a $1.4 million loan from the union pension fund in spite of the fact that the union officials had previously loaned five million dollars to the same interests and that that loan had been defaulted. By way of collateral on this second "loan," two defendants represented to the union officials the acquisition of an impressive array of subcontracts. The indictment suggested that these representations were ridiculous.

The point of the scheme was allegedly to milk the pension fund of money and spread it around among various underworld figures involved. The seven men indicted in this case were Irwin Weiner, a former Chicago bailbondsman and an associate of the late Murray Humphreys, whom you are about to meet; Ronald de Angeles, a "wire man" (electronic bugging expert) for the underworld; Anthony Spillotro, a leading underworld figure in Chicago and a close associate of the late Phillip Alderisio; Joseph Lombardo, also a Chicago underworld figure; Allen Dorfman, former financial executive of the Teamsters' Union, associate of Weiner's, and recent alumnus of a federal penitentiary, where he had served a term for kickbacks in connection with a pension fund loan; Jack Sheetz, a trustee of the pension fund from Dallas; and Albert Matheson, a Detroit lawyer and trustee of the pension fund. In addition, the indictment charged that union funds had turned up as far away from Chicago as Las Vegas, in various casinos and hotels, and in the bank accounts of the Anthony Stewart Gift Shop in the Circus Hotel. The gift shop is owned by Anthony Spillotro, and was allegedly used as a mechanism for laundering money from the pension fund. (At this writing, the government's case against these seven defendants had not yet been brought to trial.)

For professional criminals, union racketeering is a choice trade. Not surprisingly, it has attracted some of the underworld's outstanding talent. This has been the recruitment pattern, in fact, since the origin of racketeering in Chicago in the wake of repeal of Prohibition.

The master performer was Murray ("The Camel") Humphreys.

He was a former Capone machine-gunner turned clandestine power in Chicago's cleaning and dyeing industry, as well as in the linen-supply business and the laundry trade. He controlled the truck drivers and in-house employee unions of these industries.

He had a fearsome reputation in Chicago, but to the public he presented a figure as cheerful and dapper as Mickey Cohen's. An expensive, tasteful dresser, he was commonly seen around town in an expensive camel's hair coat (from which, the appellation "The Camel"), and a late-model car.* His well-appointed apartment featured expensive art work and Oriental rugs on the floor. All of his bathrooms were done up in a regal-red color scheme, including the private bathroom for his pet chow dog. One of the rooms in his fourteen-room apartment was converted into a rifle range. In his later years The Camel quietly purchased a lavish residence on Harbor Drive in Key Biscayne, Florida, a few blocks from where former President Nixon was later to establish himself.

Murray Humphreys was also active in converting the Chicago underworld over to the post-Prohibition economy. As the bootlegging business declined in the wake of legalization of liquor, the Capone gang desperately sought a way of utilizing all their trucks and platoons of truck drivers. It was The Camel who came up with the bright idea of simply moving into the milk delivery business, where trucks and drivers were useful things to have.

First, however, The Camel needed to control the relevant unions. This turned out to be not the piece of cake he had hoped for. Resistance among established union leaders was strong, and Humphreys' initial efforts were rebuffed.

One day in early 1932 The Camel, decked out as usual in his finest, and Frank Diamond, a relative of Al Capone, paid a courtesy call on the leader of the Milk Wagon Drivers' Union. The leader was Steve C. Sumner, eighty-four years of flint and determination. Sumner had spearheaded the counterattack on The Camel's organization drive, and had even appeared as a key prosecution witness at a racket conspiracy trial of Capone hoods alleged to have

---

* "Or it may derive from his last name: he was also known as "The Hump."

sought to muscle in on the one million dollars in cash sitting in the milk wagon union's treasury.

At the trial, Sumner testified that on this day "Humphreys said that he and others were about to start the Meadowmoor Dairy. He said my union should let him alone for six weeks until he had his dairy filled up with customers at cut-rate prices.

"He said that after six weeks we could call a strike and then he would be able to say that his organization had to pay the union scale and would have to raise the price of milk. He said to me, 'All you lose is your take for six weeks or two months.'

"I asked him what he meant by 'take' and he said, 'rake-off.' I told him that we never took a penny from the milk dealers. I asked Humphreys why he was bothering us. I said we had a clean, decent union.

"Humphreys replied the Prohibition racket would soon be over and that they wanted a place to put their men. He said, 'The milk business looks good to me.'

"He told me his outfit owned judges, Congressmen, the police, and the State's Attorney's office. He said that if any of his men got in trouble in any part of the country all they had to do was to call him and they would be out in two hours."

Sumner said that he told Humphreys that gang gorillas would not look totally comfortable on the driver's seats of milk wagons. He said the underworld figure replied that the gang did not intend to make drivers out of the hoodlums, but to use them to collect bills and solicit trade, perhaps by machine guns and bombs.

After this talk with Humphreys, according to Sumner, the union officials fortified the union headquarters with armor plate, hired bodyguards, and took other security measures to protect the place from frontal gang assault. None was forthcoming, however. Sumner's sensational testimony at the trial and the resultant publicity scared Humphreys off, and he left the union alone. Other gangsters tried to do business with Sumner, though. One pair came to Sumner in January of 1939 and offered to assassinate Humphreys for $30,000. "We'll bring you his eye and ear," one of them said to Sumner. Sumner turned them down.

Humphreys lost this minor battle in his struggle to seize control of certain unions, but in the end he emerged as the leading underworld figure in the Chicago union movement. His was an all-out effort. To Humphreys, and to other progressive-thinking gangsters, unions were a vital and powerful factor in American life that professional criminals could not ignore. As he once put it to an official of the Bartender's Union in Chicago:

"Why don't you have some sense," he said to George B. McLane. "You have been in the labor game all your life, you ain't got a quarter, you have a home and a mortgage on it, what have you got?"

McLane's reply was: "What have I got? I can go to sleep at night and put my head on a pillow and I don't have to smoke a pipe to go to sleep, and I ain't going to push nobody around for you or for anyone else."

Humphreys' comeback was truly a memorable one: "That's your trouble. We call it business, and you call it pushing people around."

They are still pushing people around. For example, there was once an American firm having trouble with a local union. In desperation, it turned to a well-known racketeer with labor connections. The company paid him $15,000 as a consultant. The firm had no more union trouble. In a noted extortion case, a union secretary-treasurer indicated to a large trucking firm that $5,000 would buy unfettered access to Kennedy International Airport in New York. In another case, an investigation revealed that one local union, controlled by criminals, had referred for employment to a company with which it did business applicants of such dubious background that fully half of them failed rudimentary credit and criminal-background checks. Yes, they are still pushing people around, but now it's a very big business.

Just how big a business is illustrated by an unusually detailed story about a behind-the-scenes criminal who controlled a great deal of the New York area meat business.

In a hotel room in New York a few years ago, Currier J. Holman and other desperate officials of the powerful Iowa Beef Processors, Inc., decided to face reality. They reluctantly came to the conclusion, after considerable anguish, that if they wanted to sell their boxed beef in the New York market, they would have to deal with a shadowy figure named Moe Steinman. So they picked up the phone and called him.

The fateful phone call followed years of frustration and near financial collapse for Iowa Beef. As pieced together by Jonathan Kwitney of the *Wall Street Journal,* the story vividly illustrates how professional criminals in control of labor unions were able to bring even powerful executives of Iowa Beef, the largest beef packer in the world and the 117th-largest industrial company in the world, to their knees.

The key underworld figure in this story was Moe Steinman. Like Meyer Lansky, he was not much to look at, certainly not a terrific dresser, and roughly Lansky's height. He had another Lansky attribute, however: in his particular sphere of influence he was not to be crossed.

The story began in 1969. Iowa Beef officials invented a boxed-beef method of shipping meat products to New York. A new plant was built to handle the new packaging technique, which eliminated one step in the long march of beef from the slaughterhouse to the shopper's cart. The innovation should have saved money for the consumers. Because of Moe Steinman, exactly the opposite was the result.

The moment Iowa Beef moved into its new installation, the Amalgamated Meat Cutters and Retail Food Stores Employees Union struck the Midwestern company. It was a long, vicious, violent strike. "They burnt our general counsel's house to the ground," Currier Holman told two prosecuting attorneys, in a tape recording admitted into evidence in the trial. "It was intended to be my house, which is immediately contiguous to his, but they just missed."

At the height of the union-management struggle, Holman received an unsolicited phone call from New York. The voice at the other end of the line was Benny Moscowitz's. Holman vaguely remembered him as a New York meat wholesaler he had met years ago.

Holman had no way of knowing it at the time, but Moscowitz was now fronting for Moe Steinman, the master underworld fixer, New York's contemporary version of Murray Humphreys.

Moscowitz suggested to Holman that he knew of some people in New York who might be able to help him out of his predicament with the Meat Cutters (who felt directly threatened by the boxed-beef technique of packing).

The first get-together was held in Iowa. "And so we're sitting in the middle of the lobby of a motel," Holman recalled, "and I said [to Moe Steinman] 'What are you? What's your business? What do you want to talk about?' " It was Holman's first contact with Steinman, an unprepossessing man whom Holman later described as looking like a weasel.

Said Steinman, "Er, I do a number of things."

Steinman explained that he was vice-president of labor relations for Daitch-Shopwell supermarkets, and a partner, at the same time, in Trans-World Fabricators, a meat brokerage that acted as middleman between meat wholesalers and New York retail outlets. What Moe Steinman didn't say directly at first was that he was the answer, the costly answer, to Iowa Beef's union difficulties.

Holman then said, "We're trying to sell a lot of meat to the chain stores. Maybe you can help us out." Then, according to Holman, Steinman said, "Maybe I can."

By the spring of 1970, with the strike still continuing, Iowa Beef's creditors were threatening to foreclose on loans and credit lines. In April, Holman and other top executives went to New York for another go-round with Moe Steinman.

In a room in the Stanhope Hotel, Holman bluntly appealed to Steinman for help.

The next day, Steinman produced high-ranking officials and attorneys of the butchers' union. They met in a Stanhope room that was "very dark, and (it was) difficult to see the people . . . The blinds were closed," according to Holman's recollection.

At one point a union official reiterated that Steinman was "a person who could help. . . . His influence was with meat people and union people."

After further talking, a deal was made. Iowa Beef pledged to pay Steinman's brokerage firm 25 cents on every one hundred pounds of boxed beef sold in a 125-mile radius of Columbus Circle, roughly the geographic center of New York. For his part, Steinman pledged help in ending the strike. (At a dinner held that night to toast the deal, Steinman allegedly boasted to Holman that he paid off butchers' union officials the first Tuesday of every month.)

A month later, after beef officials had returned to Iowa believing that their troubles were over, Steinman upped the ante. He said his people now required fifty cents per hundred pounds. Holman screamed.

"Look, I need the fifty cents," Steinman reportedly claimed, "I got to buy a steward. . . . I've got to buy a guy a broad. I may have to buy a chain store buyer. I've got to pay cash."

A few months later Steinman brought up the 50-cent commission again. "I asked him what for," recalled Holman, "and he said, 'Well, I have other expenses. . . . There are three kinds. I pay meat buyers off at fifteen percent. I pay union people off at seven percent. And it costs me ten percent to convert corporate money to cash,* and I have to deal in cash.' "

A final compromise was reached: Fifty cents per one hundred pounds for the first five million pounds of boxed beef, then thirty-five cents above that.

Under the new deal, Steinman's brokerage firm was guaranteed a minimum payoff of $25,000 a month.

As a bonus to Steinman, Iowa Beef agreed to retain a certain attorney as a consultant at $25,000 a year. And who was this attor-

---

* Ten percent is the standard underworld commission for laundering money. Steinman would filter payoff money through a "respectable" bank before it reached union officials to disguise the source of the funds.

ney? According to testimony, Holman had once been warned by a colleague in the meat industry about Steinman—"You probably may have to hire his son-in-law in the bargain. . . ."

Shortly after Iowa Beef was back in business and the strike was mysteriously halted, sixteen federal and state indictments were filed against Steinman and other racketeers, beef officials and union officers, on various counts of conspiracy, bribery and income tax evasion. Even after the indictments, however, Moe Steinman remained king of the New York meat business. He was able to dictate to supermarket chains what they would display on their counters. As this book went to press, the case against Steinman had not come to trial.

In another matter under investigation, an executive of Food-O-Rama, an East Coast chain, stopped buying from a Steinman-controlled brokerage. An associate of Steinman's called soon thereafter to remind officials of Food-O-Rama about their upcoming contract negotiations with a meat local. Steinman's name turned up in the conversation. Perhaps Steinman would help with the negotiations, the associate added, a likelihood that might be enhanced if the chain were to drop the new brand of beef patties (Frozen Queen) and reorder from Steinman's client. The chain thought it over and reversed its cancellation of the Steinman order. For his part, Steinman dealt directly with the appropriate union officials. Everything turned up rosy.

Steinman is typical of the new behind-the-scenes "white collar" professional criminal. With his contacts in the criminal world—a frequent dinner companion was labor racketeer John (Johnny Dio) Dioguardi—Steinman wheeled and dealt with New York locals like a sculptor molding clay. Over the years Steinman's carefully constructed power base made him the indispensable fixer for a number of firms in the meat industry.

Moe Steinman is the kind of figure commentators have in mind when they speak of professional criminals going legitimate. For on the face of it, he was nothing more than an official for a respected supermarket chain and a brokerage house that was listed, like any other business, in the Yellow Pages.

But under Steinman, the meat trade in New York was anything but a business as usual. According to some estimates, racketeering in the New York area meat industry adds from one to five cents to the retail price of each pound of meat sold in the city. This means that meat racketeering is a tremendously profitable business. On the Iowa Beef deal alone, had prosecutors not moved in, Steinman's brokerage house would have netted $600,000 a year. And Iowa Beef Inc. was just one of dozens of meat firms forced to do business with Moe Steinman.

CHAPTER TEN

Future Crime

WHEN MEYER LANSKY was just starting out in the streets of Brooklyn, police officers used bicycles most of the time to get to the scene of the crime. There just wasn't money in the city budget for enough Model-T's to go around.

The young Lansky saw an opening. Before long, he had organized his own rent-a-car firm—only, the company wasn't legally incorporated and the cars weren't legally acquired. Soon gangs throughout Brooklyn were renting hot cars from the young Meyer, in the process leaving the Brooklyn cops pedaling breathlessly behind.

The law is still trying to catch up. Since Meyer Lansky's days as a youth, American society has witnessed the rise and encrustation of a permanent professional-criminal class. In the war on crime, the bad guys are ahead.

The spoils of war include considerable economic and political leverage over legitimate American society and great personal wealth for the leaders of the profession. It would be interesting to compare the personal fortune of, say, Nelson Rockefeller with that of Meyer Lansky. Who's worth more? The very fact that such a question can even be reasonably asked is itself revealing.

The criminal profession is not a pessimistic one. A professional criminal never believes *he* will be caught, though he is prepared for the worst. Nor does he entertain the slightest fear that there will be no place for the kind of thing he does in America's future.

The present has been prologue. The continuity of tradition assures the criminal that only certain revisions, not major surgery, will be required in the first nine chapters of this book. The things he does seem ageless. Technological changes and advances in American society will not shut him out. If the burglary of a safe demands laser technology, the professional criminal, if the deal is worth it, will obtain the necessary tools. If the fence will require computer printouts of inventory to keep abreast of the latest changes in lists, he'll make a friend in the computer room.

Today's criminal is allied with the best technical help money can buy. Computers, which service banks, credit-card companies and collection agencies, are clearly the keys to the kingdom. With increasing frequency, they are used as the silent partner of the criminal. Programs can be stolen, computer time can be borrowed, input data can be fudged or manipulated, output data can be falsified; all it takes is an inside man. A study prepared by the United States Chamber of Commerce concluded that "the chief weakness of computer systems is people." Of those incidents of criminal misuse of computer systems that have come to the attention of the law, the dollar loss has been as high as five million dollars per incident.

At an underworld conclave in Atlantic City in 1931, Meyer Lansky warned crime bosses from all over the country not to fall victims of their success. As he spoke the nation was in the process of repealing Prohibition. Lansky's concern was that the profession not be left behind the times. He told his peers that crime had to expand into such then-virgin areas as unions, real estate, banking, and so on, before it was too late. More than forty years ago, then, Lansky correctly foresaw the need for professional criminals to go into so-called white collar crime.*

* Essentially, the term "white collar" crime is regrettable. In my view, it is the product of class snobbery, and is the Edsel of criminological terminology. Let us say the socially connected president of a prestigious savings

A great deal of future crime will wear the camouflage of the white collar. In addition to computer-related crime, the professional will undertake operations in such areas as consumer fraud (e.g., phony work-at-home opportunities, going-out-of-business sales that last an eternity, home "repairs," bait-and-switch advertising), embezzlement, securities fraud and theft, and insurance fraud.

There is already some evidence to suggest that the future is now. As of mid-'73, there were some 400,000 lost, stolen or missing securities worth $5.3 million reported to police. (Because of the inadequacy of reporting procedures, it is believed that this represents at best 10 percent of the actual total.) Over the past twenty years roughly one hundred banks in the United States have been forced to close because of fraudulent schemes perpetrated by professionals.

On the interface between so-called blue collar crime and white collar crime, the professional criminal will simply switch collars like a politician changing his tune for different audiences. One recent indictment in New York illustrates what has been happening. The defendant was a fifty-seven-year-old man who lived at 219 Mulberry Street, which is located in the heart of Little Italy in New York. This section of the city has produced more than its share of professional criminals. The defendant was indicted on two separate charges. The first was attempting to sell $200,000 in hijacked goods. The second was attempting to sell $2.6 million in stolen securities. Obviously, the difference between a hijacker and a stolen-securities operator is perhaps *only* one of collars.

---

and loan institution is indicted and convicted on a charge of stock fraud, manipulation and theft. So we call the act a white collar crime. But if the same sort of crime is committed by an Italian-American Mafioso who used to make his living by hijacking trucks, then we call it something else. But the act is the same, whether the perpetrators wear blue collars or white! On top of this, the term obscures the additional fact that the so-called white collar criminals are increasingly allied with the blue collars on many of these criminal ventures. Why is the fence a blue collar criminal and his receivers lily-white? Why is the man who hijacks a truckload of shrimp with a pistol inferior, in some sense of terminology, to the manufacturer who robs the public with his defective products?

The professional criminal simply wears whatever kind of collar makes him the most money. He will dress up in a tuxedo to rob the safety-deposit boxes of a luxury hotel, or dress down in repairman's coveralls to look like a professional blue-collar worker.

Even blue-collar crime can have a white-collar ring to it. In one scheme that will be increasingly common in the future, elements of both styles are present. This scheme involves abuse of the holder-in-due-course doctrine governing loan agreements. A home-repair firm advertises repairs and improvements on the installment plan. Your roof is deteriorating, your bankbook is virtually depleted, so you call the firm and wind up signing an installment contract with the home-repair firm to keep the roof from falling in.

Within a few days, you receive a letter from a finance company you never heard of demanding immediate payment of the entire loan. What has happened is that the blue-collar repair outfit has pulled a white-collar trick: it has sold your installment contract to the finance company, which, under the holder-in-due course doctrine, has the right to demand the remaining payments. Of course, as you are reading the letter from the finance company, the roof has not been worked on.

And don't bother calling the firm; it has already pulled up stakes and vanished, leaving in its wake hundreds of others like yourself in the community the victims of this white-and-blue collar crime.

Like many future crimes, this one will work best when the economy is worst. For example, another tight-money racket depends completely on the desperation of small businessmen. It is known as the advance-fee racket, and it begins with the appearance of an advertisement in a financial newspaper indicating the availability of loan money for small businesses. The ad will contain an impressive financial prospectus of the lending institution, which in reality is nothing more than a store-front corporation located, possibly, in some small Caribbean country.

The small businessman will apply for the loan through one of the

American agents listed on the advertisement. Under the terms of the loan agreement (he is informed by the broker) the applicant is required as a token of good faith to pay an advance fee of, say, 10 percent of the face value of the loan note. The small businessman delivers his token. The loan firm does not.

In the weeks to follow, the businessman receives (1) fake documents about how the loan is being processed; (2) a letter indicating that before the loan can be advanced the businessman's company must be further investigated; or (3) various excuses for the delay. In effect, what the businessman receives is a stall. What he never receives, of course, is the loan. His legal recourse is slim indeed. As a foreign corporation, the "loan company" is relatively invulnerable to accountability to nationals of another country.

Lucrative rackets of the future will exploit the growing vulnerability of the American small-businessman and consumer caught in the maelstrom of the American economy. The strategy will involve the mirage of appearing to fill in shortage gaps. Whether the shortage is meat or gasoline, wheat or dollars, the racket will exploit the demand situation by appearing to be the supplier.

What is easily predicted is that the loan sharks are in a tremendous position to enhance their leverage in the future. The criminals with money to lend will attain tremendous economic clout over the small-business community. By the time the economy rights itself, the professionals will have burrowed their way into so many American small businesses as to blur beyond all recognition in the future the traditional distinction between organized crime and legitimate business. In many cases, the two will become cousins.

In the future, the crime world will open its doors to the kinds of Americans who years ago would perhaps not even have thought of entering on such a career.

The most promising possibility, in the perverse sense of "promising," is the involvement of female Americans in crime. The traditional *macho* of the American male criminal has long held women back, but there is now every reason to believe that women may be ready to make their big move into crime.

Until now, American women have been relegated to the most menial jobs in the underworld. They have been limited largely to prostitution and other forms of undercover work (compromising clients, police officers, competitors and so on).

But nothing in the essentials of the business logically excludes the possibility of professional performance by women. There is nothing in the nature of most of the rackets described in the previous chapters that cannot be mastered by women. Their relative exclusion from crime, then, can be attributed to the very same factors that account for female exclusion or underrepresentation in other professions—i.e., social conditioning, choice and male opposition.

The most promising area for female crime is narcotics. There is simply no reason why a female trafficking team could not be put together. Indeed, one small one that I know of already exists. It is an East Coast outfit, and it operates a cocaine run from Latin America to Miami and New York. Its members include stewardesses, high school teachers, nurses and actresses. Most of the girls in the ring come from respectable middle-class families (that is, their parents are not criminals), and look as straight as Brenda Starr. Some of them graduated from good colleges and universities, and are even active in local politics and social activities. Much of the coke that is brought in is consumed by the girls and their boyfriends, but some of it is sold at regular market prices to their peers in the professions. It is certainly not a multibillion-dollar-a-year operation, but as a pilot project it definitely shows promise.

The full potential of women in crime has hardly been touched. In one celebrated case in Los Angeles—trivial, perhaps, but still illuminating—a teen-age girl and a male accomplice stuck up a number of West Coast banks. The girl showed up at the bank with a pistol, a see-through blouse, and no bra. When questioned later by police, all eyewitnesses were embarrassed by their failure to have concentrated on her facial features.

On a more consequential level, female Americans are conspicuously well-qualified for the so-called white-collar crimes of fraud and bankruptcy. In the latter crime, a female American makes for an ideal "pencil," because, among other things, she is likely to be convincing in the role of innocent victim of tragic circumstances beyond her control and, besides, probably won't have a criminal record.

Female Americans constitute a huge pool of previously unarrested potential criminals.* In the kind of crime in which an absolutely clean background is a prerequisite, their use will be valuable. The lack of a criminal record will also help explain the growing success of new ethnic-Americans in crime. A great many Italian-American, Jewish, Irish and black professionals, even successful ones, have arrest records that make them prime suspects for almost any serious professional crime in their locale, or area of specialization. But a recent Cuban-American, Chinese, South American or Arabic immigrant—to mention just a few examples—starts out with a clean slate, even if he or she may have been deeply involved in the rackets of the home country.

This is a tremendous advantage. At a time when the average top-level Mafioso can't go to the mail box without being filmed by three separate law enforcement surveillance teams (each one unaware of the other's presence), comparable high-level non-Italian criminals can operate in relative obscurity. The opening-up of America's immigration policies after 1965 has been a tremendous boon to the rise of black and brown professional crime.

The infusion of new faces into crime has made for a more confused profession. The central core of crime in America remains professionalized, but the ranks of the peripheral areas have swollen dramatically in the last few years. In a sense, crime in America is getting less organized. The democratization of the lower ranks of the crime world is creating chaos. Law-and-order in the underworld is breaking down.

---

* It is no more difficult for female Americans to perform at creditable levels in crime than to perform in law enforcement. One reason for this is that crime is no more violent than police work (and, possibly, even less so). Police officers by and large (despite the popular conception) rarely use their pistols. Criminals, by and large, are in a comparable situation. The use of force in both professions is dramatically overemphasized.

Nowhere is this more obvious than in the nation's cities, where the average age of the young criminal adventurer seems to lower each year at the same time that the involvement of young people in crime seems to increase. In New York City, according to recent data, crime ordinarily attributable to youth is dramatically on the rise. Rape arrests were up 33 percent in 1974 over the previous year. Assaults increased 13 percent. Robbery rose 5 percent. Although figures in other cities are not available, there is reason to believe that it is a nationwide pattern.

The growing involvement of very young people in crime is a very frightening sign of things to come. The lowering average age of the young criminal has the effect of deprofessionalizing the profession. Young people are as a rule the least stable, most violence-prone of all criminals. Their primary arena is the street, and their primary target is defenseless people like you and me.

This growing phenomenon seems out of the control of the professionals. In many areas of our cities where organized crime families were entrenched—especially Chinese and Italian crime families—street crime was virtually nonexistent. The professionals wanted to operate in relative isolation from the police, as well as to keep their communities under control; so they policed their communities themselves. Today the young people have taken over the streets, and the nation verges on hysteria.

This is not to suggest that professional crime has not been a contributing cause of street crime. The very existence of a profitable, powerful criminal profession is one of the incentives that drive young people into the streets to commit crime, not to mention the failure of the nation's criminal-justice system to cope with the problem. As the President's National Crime Commission observed, "For good or for evil, the law and its failure teach. People know when crime pays. Kids in the slums see the cop on the beat taking money. They know the pusher seldom gets caught, and his wholesaler is virtually never touched. They learn this lesson better than any middle-class values taught in the schools from which they drop out."

The recruitment activity of professional criminals used to have a dampening effect on street violence. In an effort to impress elders with their sophistication, youths were encouraged to emulate the professionals. The rewards were assimilation into the profession. This means an emphasis on smart money crimes. But the breakdown on the hold of professionals over street crime parallels the breakdown of parental authority in society at large, and the country is going through a tremendously frightening violent-crime wave as a result.

There will always be a great deal of crime in America. As the American novelist Raymond Chandler has written, "Crime isn't a symptom, it's a disease. . . . We're a big, rough, rich, wild people, and crime is the price we pay for it, and organized crime is the price we pay for organization. We'll have it with us for a long time. Organized crime is just the dirty side of the sharp dollar."

The techniques of professional crime have paid off for the professionals. Is there any reason why they cannot be used by other Americans, with different motivations?

In future crime, this will be very much the case. As people realize how crime pays, people who are primarily motivated not by the sharp dollar, but by other desires, will take up the trade. Idealists, romantics and true revolutionaries will be encouraged to dabble in professional crime, because of the anticipated payoff.

In narcotics, there is already some evidence that politically motivated traffickers are heavily involved. To bankroll their causes, according to informed sources, some members of outfits like the Japanese Red Army, the Black Muslims and former supporters of the late Chilean President Salvador Allende may have engaged in narcotics transactions.

This should not be surprising. Political partisans often get carried away with their cause, believing that the end justifies any means. That narcotics should have attracted them is hardly surprising, in view of the profit margins involved. What is perhaps surprising is that the professionals have permitted radicals to become involved. This is either evidence of the loss of control by professionals over some areas of the business, or perhaps just of the enormous size of the narcotics trade itself—or both.

In the future, changes in the law will revise the definition of criminality, just as repeal of Prohibition converted former bootleggers into respectable businessmen of the liquor industry.

Perhaps, then, the answer to the crime problem is a change in the law. This is fine as far as it goes. Legalization of marijuana, for example, will convert grass traffickers into legitimate businessmen and pot consumers into smokers of name brands. Other drugs might be legalized; and even prostitution might be opened up, in view of the inevitability of the practice. But no matter how hard our legislators may try, it will be impossible to *legalize* the crime profession.

How can society justify the legalization of contract killing? Or the corruption of police and public officials? Or the use of force to enter private homes, the use of a weapon against a truck driver, the bribing of a computer operator to defraud a bank?

There are limits to liberalization. Besides, every society has a right to define itself in terms of approved and disapproved activity. It has a right to declare certain activities against the law. But if even one of these can be made into a profit-making enterprise, then there you have it: a criminal class. Perhaps it is not quite as simple as that, but the truth is very close.

There is no escaping the criminal. He follows us everywhere. For some time people thought they could escape the criminal by moving to the suburbs. It was wishful thinking.

In a recent Gallup poll, one out of every five suburbanites revealed that he or she had been a victim of a mugging, a robbery, a vandalism or a burglary. In the first three months of 1974, according to the Federal Bureau of Investigation, while crime in the cities rose 10 percent, crime in the suburbs increased 22 percent. The losses incurred in residential burglaries and larcenous theft in 1972 alone came to more than $940 million. This is a conservative estimate.

As the nation's wealth moved out to the suburbs, so did the professional criminal. While violent crimes in suburbia are still relatively infrequent, compared to urban averages, crimes against property have risen dramatically. This means that the professional criminal has gotten to the suburbanite first, before the amateur. This is not surprising. The professional is smarter. But it means that the amateur is not far behind.

There is no escaping the criminal. He is everywhere. A man gets up in the morning to go to work. He is a typical American. He goes to the bathroom to shave. He turns on the radio to listen to the news. A gang of muggers the night before attacked a young man riding a new imported bicycle, killed the man, and took the new bike. The man thinks to himself as he shaves how he will sand down the finish of his new bike to make it look old and worthless.

He goes into the kitchen and as he slaps a slice of bacon into the frying pan he notices that this is his last slice. The price of bacon has gone up at the butcher's, and his wife has cut back the quantity. The price went up because the local butcher's union, controlled by criminals, recently raised its payoffs to union and management figures, who passed the increased cost off to the butcher. And he passed it off to the typical American.

He goes to his desk to write out a few checks before leaving for work. First, there is the insurance premium, due quarterly. The house is insured not only for fire, but for theft. The premium is higher this year than last because of a rash of burglaries in the neighborhood. Then there is insurance for the car. It is higher this year because big-engine Chevrolets were a hot item last year for car thieves. The man owns a big-engine Chevy. Then there is the monthly garage fee. The insurance company wouldn't even sell the man theft insurance unless he garaged the car. The man thinks,

Everybody's making money off crime except me—even the owner of the parking garage!

He opens his front door to pick up his morning newspapers, but they are gone. An adolescent has organized a newspaper-theft ring and is reselling them three blocks away. He walks into the parking garage a few blocks away and asks for his car. The attendant looks for the keys but they are gone. There was a new boy on last night, he says, as the two of them frantically search the garage for the car, which is now in the hands of a car-theft ring. The new boy, of course, never shows up for work that night. The man goes to work by cab, consoling himself along the way with the thought that, at least, the car was insured for theft.

At work the man, a bank loan officer, has to write out default papers on a loan to a small candy store in town. The candy store is going out of business. It is unable to compete with the candy store across the street. One reason it can't is that its competitor is selling untaxed cigarettes. They were smuggled into the state by professional criminals. The man remembers a representative from the D.A.'s office telling him that in the last four months of last year alone, over one hundred cigarette retail outlets in New York went out of business because of competition from outlets selling smuggled, untaxed cigarettes at lower prices.

At work he calls a body shop where his wife's car is being repaired. For the first time that day, the man hears good news. The owner of the garage tells him that the car will be ready tomorrow. We got a real break on the front-end part, the owner says, and the price we got for you, it's a real steal.

At lunch the man goes to a restaurant around the block. After dessert, he goes to the men's room. The men's room is absolutely filthy. It looks like the place has never been cleaned. Why haven't the Board of Health people been here to inspect? he thinks. Actually, they were there, but only to collect payoffs for ignoring the sanitary conditions of the restaurant, which is owned by organized-crime figures.

The man goes back to work. That afternoon an emergency meeting of the bank officers is held. The vice-president in charge of the bank announces that Fred X., a long-time employee, is no longer with the firm. An FBI investigation caught him in the act of selling the bank's computer program to organized-crime figures. Further investigation revealed that the bank employee was deep in debt to a loan shark and was trying to pay the debt off with an inside job.

Shaken, the man goes back to his desk. He reads the afternoon paper and sees that the point spread on Sunday's football game is only three points. He picks up the phone and calls his bookie. He places the bet on credit.

Later that afternoon the man is sitting in his office, and a secretary from another department walks in. She is young and very good-looking. She inquires whether the deal is the same for tomorrow night. The deal is always the same: the girl adds fifty dollars to her income every week with this deal.

The man leaves the office early to go to a local bar. Along the way he is hustled by a junkie for some change in his pocket. In comparison to what's happened so far it's not even a drop in the bucket.

At the bar he sits down and orders a dry Martini. It has, after all, been an unusually rough day. The Martini costs a dollar more. Only last week it was just a dollar. The man is about to say something to the bartender, but decides not to. What the man doesn't know is that last week the bar was owned by one person; this week there are two owners. The new owner is a loan shark. It is now an organized crime bar.

The bartender tells the man that there is some complimentary fresh shrimp over at the condiment table. The man doesn't know it, but the shrimp were hijacked just the night before on the other side of town. The man sits at the bar enjoying the shrimp. He is both the victim and accomplice of the criminal.

He goes home that night and watches television. There is a singer on a talk show. He cannot understand how a person of such little talent can make it to a national television show. He doesn't know that the producer is a good friend of a criminal with a lot of influence in the record industry. He catches the late news show. A politician running for governor says that if elected he will stamp out the criminal. The man tries to fall asleep.

ACKNOWLEDGMENTS

HERE IS a list of the people who helped me with this book whose names I can disclose:

In New York, Frank Hubert and Phil Crepeau of the New York Police Department's Auto Crime Unit (whose week-long course in auto theft I was apparently the first civilian to attend); Peter Truebner, Assistant United States Attorney for the Southern District of New York; Jerry Jenson, of the United States Drug Enforcement Administration; William Bonacum, retired chief of the N.Y.P.D.'s Narcotics Squad; Paul Herny, James Cunningham, Carl Galena, Bob Hernandez, Martin Butler, and Aaron Grossman of the Safe, Loft and Truck Squad of the N.Y.P.D.; John Kid, the department's expert on locks and safes; John Welsome, of the N.Y.P.D.'s gambling squad; Maurice Nadjari and his aide William Federici for their views on corruption and crime; Ralph Salerno, of the Queens D.A. office; Mario Merola, the Bronx D.A.; Frank Rogers, special narcotics prosecutor; and William McCarthy, former Deputy Commissioner of Police.

In Chicago, Steven A. Schiller of the Chicago Crime Commission; Sheldon Davidson, former Attorney-in Charge of the Chicago strike force; his successor David Schippers, and *his* successor Peter Vaira, the present boss; and Eugene Eidenberg, chairman of the Illinois Law Enforcement Commission; and the library of the *Chicago Tribune,* and clip file of the Chicago bureau of the Los Angeles *Times.*

In Philadelphia, Assistant United States Attorney Thomas Bergstrom, among others.

In Los Angeles, Sergeant J. M. Scherrer of the intelligence division of the L.A.P.D.; Mickey Cohen, the racketeer and his valet,

Jimmy Smith; Ed Guthman, national editor of the Los Angeles *Times;* the library of the *Times;* and John Kelly, former federal narcotics agent and presently a private investigator with offices on Sunset Strip.

In Washington, William Durkin, Jerry Strickler, and Con Dougherty of the Federal Drug Enforcement Administration; John Dowd and R. J. Campbell (who has since resigned) of the Organized Crime and Racketeering section of the U.S. Department of Justice; and Telly Kossack and Bill Lynch of the National District Attorney's Association's economic crime center.

In Miami, special agent Peter Scrocca of D.E.A.; assistant United States Attorney Howard Keefe; and the library of the Miami *News.*

Other persons who were tremendously helpful in various ways include Joan Sanger, Patrick Mann, Fritz Ianni, Jerry Lubenow, Will Ramsey, Rose Nevins, Sally Jesse, Jack Nugent (who coauthored the recent—and splendid—biography of Mickey Cohen), Richard Matheson, and Martha and Bryce Nelson, to whom I am indebted for suggesting the title.

Finally, and perhaps most importantly for their professional encouragement, Theron Raines and Michael Korda.

It took the cooperation of many professional criminals to prepare this book. None of them was in prison at the time I interviewed them. This was important to me because I have always believed that convicts are the least likely source for an optimistic reading on the profession of crime.

I was fortunate in having their cooperation, which I secured through (1) the kind assistance of working gentlemen in the law-enforcement world; (2) my own contacts in the crime world; and (3) plain dumb luck.

After some preliminary circling, some bad guys talked to me at length, and as freely as prudence permitted. They opened up to the extent that they could truly believe that I was not an undercover cop, and that I would not print their names (sometimes they did not even give me their true names—which was acceptable, because I was interested in what they did, not who they were).

I met them at racetracks, restaurants, seedy night clubs, suburban parking lots. Many of them were quite kind and courteous to me. Perhaps this was just smart public relations on their part. Perhaps, too, they were responding to my attitude, which was to approach what they did for a living without taking the high moral line. Perhaps also they simply enjoyed talking freely to a stranger who they knew was reliable. I can certainly tell you this: they did enjoy talking.

I have duly kept their names and addresses out of this book. That was part of the bargain.

Notes and Bibliography

Although the primary source for this book was the experience of professional criminals and professional law-enforcement people, a number of previously published works influenced my thinking. What follows is a selective crediting.

CHAPTER ONE (*pages 11–32*)

My definition of *professional criminal* is quite close to that of "able criminal," as developed in J. A. Mack, "The Able Criminal," *British Journal of Criminology,* Vol. 12 (January 1972), pp. 44–54. Professor Mack makes a distinction between the "full-time criminal, to be seen at his most effective in the able operator, and the full-time prisoner, the archetype of the unsuccessful operator. . . . The principle . . . that full-time operators should not be considered criminals until they are proved such in a court of law is good law and will remain so for as long as the present general ignorance on the subject of full-time criminals and criminal networks continues to be unrelieved by systematic research. It may even be good practical civics, though this is arguable. But it is inevitably bad sociology." (pp. 54, 49)

For a critique of the use of the term "professional criminal," see Donald R. Cressey, *Criminal Organization,* New York, Harper Torchbooks, 1972, pp. 1–17. See also Morris L. Cogan, "The Problem of Defining a Profession," *Annals of the American Association of Political and Social Sciences,* Vol. 362 (1955) pp. 105–11.

For the notion that professional crime is related to the wealth and complexity of society, see Mary McIntosh, "Changes in the Organization of Thieving," in Stanley Cohen, ed., *Images of Deviance,* London, Penguin, 1971.

On the bootlegging epoch, see Kenneth Allsop, *The Bootleggers and Their Era,* Garden City, N.Y., Doubleday, 1961.

On the production of criminals, see John Mack, "Full-time Miscreants, Delinquent Neighborhoods and Criminal Networks," *British Journal of Sociology,* Vol. 15 (March 1972), pp. 38–52. "It is perfectly feasible to hold that the same process is at work in the production of normal criminals as operates in the manning of the ranks of sociologists, or policemen, or decision makers, or any other more respectable occupational group." The perceptive reader will notice that I have tried to avoid using the word "deviant" in connection with the professional criminal. This is because the term misleads more than it informs. However, on the sociology of deviance, a great deal of good work has been done. See, for example, Paul Rock, "The Sociology of Deviance and Conceptions of Moral Order," *British Journal of Sociology,* Vol. 14 (April 1974), pp. 139–49; Jack D. Douglas, ed., *Deviance and Respectability,* New York, Basic Books, 1970; Edwin M. Lemert, *Human Deviance, Social Problems and Social Control,* Englewood Cliffs, N.J., Prentice-Hall, 1967.

On the notion of a career in crime, see Edwin Lemert, "The Behavior of the Systematic Check Forger," *Social Problems,* Vol. 6 (Fall 1958), 141–49; and Norval Morris, *The Habitual Criminal,* Cambridge, Mass., Harvard University Press, 1951; and Howard Becker, *The Outsiders,* New York, The Free Press, 1964; and Ned Polsky, *Hustlers, Beats and Others,* Chicago, Aldine, 1967; and, a truly imaginative work, Leroy C. Gould, *et. al., Crime as a Profession,* Washington, D.C., U.S. Department of Justice, Law Enforcement Assistance, 1968. According to the last-named study, "The most striking thing about present-day relationships between professional criminals is that these relationships are not structured by strong ongoing group relationships, but are structured primarily by the crimes that professional criminals commit." (p. 32) This is to say, crime is organized, simply, out of necessity and efficiency.

A number of sociological works have focused on the individual criminal with great success. For the idea that crime is hard labor, see: Peter Letkemann, *Crime as Work,* Englewood Cliffs, N.J., Prentice-Hall, 1965. On the relationship between criminals, mental institutions and prisons, see David Biles and Glenn Mulligan, "Mad or Bad? The Enduring Dilemma," *British Journal of Sociology,* Vol. 13 (July 1973), pp. 275–79. For a discussion of the relationship between success in crime and the likelihood of repetition, see Daniel Glaser, *The Effectiveness of a Prison and Parole System,* Indianapolis, Bobbs-Merrill, 1964. For the opinion that some criminals are in it for an emotional —rather than a financial—lift, see John MacIsaac, *Half the Fun Was Getting There,* Englewood Cliffs, N.J., Prentice-Hall, 1968. And for a sense of how the body of crime knowledge is transmitted, see C. R.

Jeffry, "Criminal Behavior and Learning Theory," *Journal of Criminal Law, Criminology and Police Science,* Vol. 56 (September 1966), pp. 294–300.

On the problem of crime statistics, see Kitsuse and Cicourel, "A Note on the Uses of Official Statistics," *Social Problems,* Vol. 11 (Fall 1963), pp. 131–39. See also "The Production of Crime Rates," *American Sociological Review,* Vol. 35 (August 1970), pp. 733–47.

On measuring the cost of crime, see Robert G. Hann, "Crime and the Cost of Crime: An Economic Analysis," *Journal of Resolution in Crime and Delinquency,* Vol. 9 (January 1972), pp. 12–30.

On the subject of burglary, the following works were very useful: Neal Elwood Shover, *Burglary as an Occupation,* Urbana, University of Illinois at Urbana-Champaign (unpublished Ph.D. dissertation), 1971; and Edwin Sutherland, *The Professional Thief,* Chicago, University of Chicago Press, 1937 (this is *the* classic study of a professional criminal). On the defecation problem, see Albert B. Friedman, "The Scatological Rites of Burglars," *Western Folklore,* Vol. 27 (July 1968), pp. 171–79. On the question of risk-taking among burglars, see John Bartlow Martin, *My Life in Crime,* New York, Signet Books, 1953. "Burglary in the long run is safer [than robbery]," says Martin. "You'll get away with a hundred burglaries where you'll only get away with five stickups." And for a perception of how the police view the criminal, see Susan Black, "Burglary," *The New Yorker,* Vol. 39 (December 7 and 14, 1963), pp. 63–128, 89–152.

CHAPTER TWO (*pages 33–51*)

There is not a great deal in the scholarly literature on car theft. One of the few pieces—and it is a good one—is Leonard D. Savitz, "Automobile Theft," *Journal of Criminal Law, Criminology, and Police Science,* Vol. 50 (July 1959), pp. 132–43.

CHAPTER THREE (*pages 53–64*)

On bank robbery, see George M. Camp, "Nothing to Lose: A Study of Bank Robbery in America," New Haven, Yale University Press (unpublished Ph.D. dissertation), 1968.

On mugging, see the classic study, Morton Hunt, *The Mugging,* New York, Atheneum, 1972.

On victimology, see Stephen Schafer, *The Victim and His Criminal: A Study in Functional Responsibility,* New York, Random House, 1968.

On gangs and crime, see David J. Bordua, "Delinquent Subcultures: Sociological Interpretations of Gang Delinquency," *Annals of the American Academy of Political and Social Science,* Vol. 388 (November 1961), pp. 119–36; also, Dean E. Frease, "The Schools, Self-Concept and Juvenile Delinquency," *British Journal of Sociology,* Vol. 12 (April 1972), pp. 133–45; Richard A. Cloward and Lloyd C. Ohlin,

Delinquency and Opportunity, Glencoe, Ill., The Free Press, 1960; Albert K. Cohen, *Delinquent Boys,* New York, The Free Press, 1955; perhaps the best, David Matza, *Delinquency and Drift,* New York, John Wiley and Sons, 1964.

CHAPTER FOUR (*pages 65–85*)

The best existing English-language work on the professional fence is Carl B. Klockars, *The Professional Fence,* New York, The Free Press, 1974. See also the pioneering work, Jerome Hall, *Theft, Law, and Society,* Boston, Little, Brown, 1935. Hall writes: "The only adequate approach to the criminal receiver is that which deals with him as an established participant in the economic life of society . . ."

Among the samplings of incarcerated criminals polled by Shover for his *Burglary as an Occupation,* the following occupations were reported as most common for fences: tavern owner or bartender; store or business owner; service-station owner or attendant; restaurant owner; and policeman. In the same work, the following occupations were reported as most common for tipsters (who work with the professional fence and thief): tavern owner or bartender; employee of victimized place; beautician; owner of victimized place. The role of the so-called legitimate person as a tipster to thief or fence is strongly emphasized in John Bartlow Martin, *My Life in Crime.*

CHAPTER FIVE (*pages 87–108*)

Shover, *op. cit.,* emphasizes the difficulty of estimating criminal income (p. 128): "I believe that responses to this question are subject to extreme memory biases, if not deliberate distortion. Consequently the data should be interpreted with extreme skepticism."

On the relationship of lawyers to criminal clients, see Abraham S. Blumberg, "The Practice of Law as a Confidence Game," *Law and Society Review,* Vol. 1 (June 1967), pp. 15–40.

On the need for a cozy cop-robber relationship, see David W. Maurer, *Whiz Mob,* as quoted in Cressey, *Criminal Organization:* "No criminal subculture can operate continuously and professionally without the connivance of the law."

On police corruption, the best recent work is *Final Report, Commission to Investigate Allegations of Police Corruption and the City's Anti-Corruption Procedures,* New York, The Fund for the City of New York, 1972.

On the many problems of our criminal-justice systems, see Jerome H. Skolnick, *Justice Without Trial,* New York, John Wiley and Sons, 1966.

On recidivism, see W. Buikhuisen and H. A. Hockstra, "Factors Related to Recidivism," *British Journal of Criminology,* Vol. 14 (January 1974), pp. 63–69. An excellent treatment—with perhaps inadequate attention to the primary cause of recidivism, which is the prison experience itself.

On the need to restructure the nation's criminal-justice system, see John Irwin, *The Felon,* Englewood Cliffs, N.J., Prentice-Hall, 1970.

CHAPTER SIX (*pages 109–133*)

On the drug market, see *Drug Use in America: Problem in Perspective,* Second Report of the National Commission on Marijuana and Drug Abuse, Washington, D.C., U.S. Government Printing Office, 1963.

See Irving H. Soloway, "Methadone and the Culture of Addiction," *Journal of Psychedelic Drugs,* Vol. 6 (January–March 1974), p. 95, for evidence that on those occasions when a criminal kicks his heroin habit, the crime may continue as an effort to obtain seed money.

CHAPTER SEVEN (*pages 135–143*)

On armed robbery, see Werner J. Einstadter, "The Social Organization of Armed Robbery," *Social Problems,* Vol. 17 (Summer 1969), pp. 64–82; and Everett De Baum, "The Heist: The Theory and Practice of Armed Robbery," *Harper's,* Vol. 200 (February 1950).

On the highly paid men of force, see *Killer: The Autobiography of a Hit Man by Joey,* Chicago, Playboy Press, 1973. Strangely, "Joey" devotes scant space to the actual works of violence, which raises the possibility that the professional criminal usually has other things on his mind than the hits and misses of everyday criminal life.

CHAPTER EIGHT (*pages 145–160*)

On monopolistic practices, see Thomas C. Schelling, "Economic Analysis and Organized Crime," Task Force Report: Organized Crime, Washington, D.C., President's Commission on Law Enforcement and the Administration of Justice, 1967. "The simplest explanation for a large-scale firm," Schelling writes, "in the underworld or anywhere else, is high costs of overhead. . . . Second is the prospect of monopolistic price increases . . ."

On frauds see Jonathan Kwitney, *The Fountainhead Conspiracy,* New York, Knopf, 1971.

On the confederation of crime, see Ralph Salerno and John S. Tompkins, *The Crime Confederation: Cosa Nostra and Allied Operations in Organized Crime,* Garden City, N.Y., Doubleday, 1969.

CHAPTER NINE (*pages 161–187*)

On Meyer Lansky, the only work of consequence is Hank Messick, *Lansky,* New York, G. P. Putnam's, 1971.

See Vincent Teresa's own story and accounts of life in the Mafia— Vincent Teresa, *My Life in the Mafia,* Garden City, N.Y., Doubleday, 1973.

On the subject of ethnicity and crime in the United States, see—
On Jewish crime, Robert A. Silverman, "Criminality Among Jews:
An Overview," *Issues in Criminality,* Vol. 6 (Summer 1971), pp. 1–35.
On Italian-American crime, Francis A. J. Ianni, *A Family Business:
Kinship and Social Control in Organized Crime,* New York, Russell
Sage–Basic Books, 1972; Nicholas Gage, *The Mafia Is Not an Equal
Opportunity Employer,* New York, McGraw-Hill, 1971; Robert T.
Anderson, "From Mafia to Cosa Nostra," *American Journal of Soci-
ology,* Vol. 71 (1965), pp. 302–10; Luigi Barzini, *The Italians,* New
York, Atheneum, 1964; Nicholas Pileggi, "How We Italians Discovered
America and Kept It Pure with Lots of Swell People," *Esquire,* June
1968, pp. 80–82; Gus Tyler, ed., *Organized Crime in America: A Book
of Readings,* Ann Arbor, Mich., University of Michigan Press, 1962.

CHAPTER TEN (*pages 189–202*)

On women in crime, see Dale Hoffman-Bustamante, "The Nature of
Female Criminality," *Issues in Criminality,* Vol. 8 (Fall 1973), 117–
36—"When we look at crimes in which female arrest rates are well
below their average for all crimes, we again find a close relationship to
sex roles. Women tend not to be arrested for crimes that require stereo-
typed male behavior—i.e., robbery, burglary. When they are arrested
on such crimes, it appears that they have played secondary, supportive
roles." (p. 131)

On the relationship between technological advance and crime, see
"Science in Safe-Cracking," *Scientific American,* Vol. 125A (December
1921), pp. 92–93; and on computers, see Aaron M. Kohn, "Computer Criminals," *Journal of Criminal Law, Criminology and Police
Science,* Vol. 60 (March 1969).

On an interesting treatment of white-collar crime, so-called, and the
pro, see Matthew G. Yeager, "The Gangster as White-Collar Criminal:
Organized Crime and Stolen Securities," *Issues in Criminology,* Vol.
8 (Spring 1973), pp. 49–67.

On political crime, see Charles E. Reasons, "The Politicizing of
Crime, The Criminal and the Criminologist," *The Journal of Criminal
Law and Criminology,* Vol. 64 (December 1973).

On crime as a permanent feature of American life, see Emile Durk-
heim, "Crime as a Normal Phenomenon," *The Criminal in Society,*
Leon Radzinowicz and Marvin E. Wolfgang, editors, New York, Basic
Books, 1971; and also Daniel Bell, "Crime as an American Way of
Life," *Antioch Review,* Vol. 13 (Summer 1952), pp. 146–51.

Index

ABOUT THE AUTHOR

Thomas Plate, a contributing editor at *New York* magazine, is also a frequent contributor to a number of other national publications. His specialty is the criminal justice system, police work, criminal behavior, and narcotics.

Mr. Plate was previously a writer for *Newsweek* (1968–70), the editor of the Viewpoints and Ideas sections of *Newsday,* and a senior editor at *New York* (1972–74) before joining the ranks of the magazine's writers.

Mr. Plate is a Phi Beta Kappa graduate of Amherst ('66) and holds a Master's degree in government from the Woodrow Wilson School of Public and International Affairs at Princeton University.